The Art of Practical Catholicism

Your faith guide to taking action in a post-COVID-19 world

The Art of Practical Catholicism

Your faith guide to taking action in a post-COVID-19 world

George Charle Manassa

© George Manassa 2020

All rights reserved. Except for quotations, no part of this book may be reproduced or transmitted in any form or by any means, electronic or mechanical, including photocopying, recording, uploading to the internet, or by any information storage and retrieval system, without written permission from the publisher.

PAR⊕USIA
Proclaiming the fullness of Truth

Published by Parousia Media Pty Ltd
PO Box 59 Galston, New South Wales, 2159
www.parousiamedia.com

Printed in Australia
ISBN: 9780645028577

Quoted versions of Scripture and the Catechism:
Catechism of the Catholic Church Second Edition

The Holy Bible - Revised Standard Version, Ignatius Edition, Copyright 2006 - Second Catholic Edition

Nihil Obstat:
Very Rev Wim Hoekstra LSS
Imprimatur:
+ Most Rev Vincent Long Van Nguyen OFMConv DD STL
Date: 28.07.2020

To my fiancée Akita Sanchez

Contents

Foreword	11
Introduction	15
1. Having the grace to start	23
2. Focusing on achieving salvation	26
3. Living your liturgy	28
4. How to evangelise in your workplace	31
5. How to defend your faith in any context	34
6. Sanctification of everyday work	37
7. Living as an Easter people	40
8. How to incorporate Mary into your spiritual life	43
9. Fighting daily spiritual warfare	46
10. Living your faith with good money	50
11. Passing on the faith to the next generation	53
12. How to support and encourage your bishop	56

13. Overcoming sins of the flesh	60
14. Traditional or traditionalist? Balancing tradition today	63
15. How to pray consistently	67
16. How to engage in mental prayer	70
17. Going to confession	72
18. The art of making a good confession	74
19. Checking your love levels	76
20. Effective Catholic education	79
21. Discerning your vocation	82
22. How to discern marriage	85
23. How to date Catholic style	88
24. Dating etiquette (dating secrets revealed)	91
25. Filtering out western sexualisation	94
26. Discerning a vocation to the priesthood	96
27. Discerning a consecrated or religious vocation	100
28. Discerning a life of blessed singleness	102
29. How to select a spiritual director	106
30. How to get involved and change your parish	108
31. The art of Catholic business networking	112
32. Guidelines for Catholic youth groups	115
33. Catholic cultural etiquette not to forget	118
34. Supporting Catholic homosexuals	120
35. Dressing modestly for women	123
36. Dressing like a Catholic man	127
37. Balancing your 'Church involvement'	130
38. Living true humility in all things	133
39. Making sense and living Canon Law	136
40. Always being prepared for death	139
Conclusion	142

The Ten Commandments	146
Prayer to St Michael the Archangel	147
Recommended reading	148
About The Catholic Toolbox	150
About The Rite of Manhood	152
Partners	155
Notes and Practical Resolutions	156

Foreword

Fr John Flader

In 1988 St John Paul II wrote in his Apostolic Exhortation *Christifideles Laici*:

> "It is not a question of simply *knowing* what God wants from each of us in the various situations of life. The individual must *do* what God wants, as we are reminded in the words that Mary, the Mother of Jesus, addressed to the servants at Cana: 'Do whatever he tells you' (John 2:5). However, to act in fidelity to God's will requires a *capability* for acting and *the developing of that capability*. We can rest assured that this is possible through the free and responsible collaboration of each of us with the grace of the Lord which is never lacking" (n. 58).

In *The Art of Practical Catholicism*, George Manassa has given us a manual on how to do just what Pope John Paul is asking: put our faith into practice.

Already in the New Testament St James told us that "faith by itself, if it has no works, is dead" (James 2:17). This is strong language. When we face Our Lord in the judgment, he will not ask us how much we knew about our faith, but rather how we lived it out in practice. The stakes are high and the reward is great. In the judgment, God will say to those who have deeds to show: "Come, O blessed of my Father, inherit the kingdom prepared for you from the foundation of the world; for I was hungry and you gave me food, I was thirsty and you gave me drink..." (Matthew 25:34-35).

Knowing that we ought to do something is one thing. Actually doing it is another. Often we don't know what we should do or how we should begin, and we remain as if paralysed. In *The Art of Practical Catholicism*, George Manassa has given us a valuable aid to help us get started. He has used the wise pedagogical device of suggesting three practical ways to implement the subject matter of each of the chapters of the book. There are no more excuses. If we wonder what we should do or how we should do it, here are three practical suggestions. They are easy to remember and easy to carry out.

The book does not expect the reader to make a dramatic change all at once. It realistically offers a program that leads the reader gradually up an inclined plane to a life of greater virtue and holiness.

And the book is easy to read in that the chapters are short and punchy. Excessive wordiness can be off-putting. Short chapters, on the contrary, invite reading to the end.

As in the case with other spiritual books, this book invites prayerful reflection on what we have read. If we are going to implement the suggestions, it will be very helpful to stop after each chapter and consider in prayer how we can live out the suggestions.

The book challenges the reader to get off the couch and do something positive. It depicts the present state of the world, which is dire in so many aspects, and calls for decisive action. It has an optimistic, hope-filled tone which inspires the reader to do his or her bit to go out and change the world for the better. It is not a matter of merely holding on to our faith in difficult times, but of letting our light shine so as to inspire others to follow Christ, thus building up the Church and making the world a better place.

In this connection I am reminded of a story I heard years ago from the principal of a Hobart Catholic girls' school in a graduation ceremony. When a girl was young she asked God for the grace to go out and change the world. When she got to middle age she realised she hadn't achieved her goal and she asked God for the grace at least to change her immediate surroundings. When she became old she realised she hadn't achieved that goal either and she asked God for the grace at least to change herself, aware that if she had asked God for that at the beginning she would have achieved all the rest. *The Art of Practical Catholicism* will help the reader start at least to change himself or herself.

Can we change the world? St Augustine, looking at the difficult times in which he lived, said in a sermon: "Let us live well and the times will be good. We are the times: as we live, so the times will be".

And lest we think we can do very little and we will not make much of a difference, we can heed the wise words of Edmund Burke, the 18th-century Irish political philosopher: "Nobody makes a greater mistake than he who did nothing because he could only do a little". And his perhaps better-known words: "All that is necessary for the triumph of evil is that the good do nothing".

On Easter Sunday 1987, Pope St John Paul II, speaking extemporaneously in an informal gathering, challenged a group of several thousand university students who had attended the UNIV conference that week in Rome:

> "There comes to my mind a reflection that is probably related to my forthcoming visit to England. It is from an English writer – Cardinal Newman, I think, but I am not sure – who, looking at London – a large city which, like other large cities, easily becomes de-Christianised, secularised – addressed this prayer to God: 'Give me 10 saints and I will change this city' … In human reality everything is done through man. To be sure, man, if he lets himself be led by the power of God, by the grace of God, if he walks beside God, is capable of changing the world. This is what I desire

for you: that you change the world, that you improve the world."

In *The Art of Practical Catholicism*, George Manassa has pointed out the way for us. Now it is up to each one of us to put it into practice. If we struggle to be the saints God wants us to be, we will change the world a little bit for the better.

Introduction

The Church has entered an era of crisis never seen before. The vast majority of Catholics have abandoned the faith, and what remains is similar to that of the early persecuted Church. But this is only the first dimension of the crisis. The second dimension of the crisis, as I like to call it, is the constant struggle of the catechised faithful to implement their faith on a practical level in our modern world. This is why this book has been written. Amid prayer and fasting over several Lenten seasons, I spent a metaphorical 40 days in the desert, preparing to face the world with these crucial insights into Catholic life and practical tips for taking action.

In each chapter you will find a short analysis and reflection on a particular aspect of the faith, where you can take time to digest and understand the topic fully. This is vital because we cannot simply implement an action without having both the knowledge and the appreciation of it to begin with. The knowledge of truth comes directly from the three hearts of formation: Scripture, Tradition and the Magisterium of the Church. In understanding the truth through Scripture and Tradition, unified with the teaching authority of the Magisterium, you will be set free, or liberated intellectually, in the true sense of the word. Once free, you will then be able to open both your mind and heart to God. Our hearts are vital because our human pride can often be clouded by our rational ways and intellectual pride. That is why the heart must be properly disposed in order to receive the Word of God. Let us also reflect on the fact that during the Gospel readings in the sacred liturgy, we make the sign of the cross on our foreheads, lips and hearts. To me, this is profound. As the priest or deacon is about to utter the written word of God from Scripture, we ask God to create in us a true disposition, allowing us to think, speak, and act as the Gospel speaks to us.

This is the very approach that I take in my ministry within the Church, through *The Catholic Toolbox*, my radio show, podcast and consultancy. The Word of God must first be preached in its fullness from the aforementioned sources. For one cannot love or act upon a truth of knowledge without knowing the 'why' to begin with.

This book is not intended to be a dense theological analysis of each topic discussed, but rather, I hope to shed light on truth in its simplicity. This is inspired by Our Lord himself, who, as a carpenter in his professional life, was well-versed in the simplicity and practicality of things. This made the Gospel accessible to all those who heard Him, not just in the realm of scholars and the academic elites of his time. We too, in our modern world, must take both practical and engaging approaches to learning, and you will find further elaboration on this throughout this book. Each chapter features an extract from Scripture, Tradition, a Magisterial or ecclesiastical document (re-affirming proclaimed doctrinal teachings) and a simple but rich reflection, strongly connected with the Old Testament story of Moses, when he went up the mountain and received the written tablets of the law. We hear about this in Exodus 20:18-19:

> *Now when all the people perceived the thunder and the lightning and the sound of the trumpet and the mountain smoking, the people were afraid and trembled; and they stood afar off, and said to Moses, 'You speak to us, and we will hear; but let not God speak to us, lest we die'.*

This was a very serious time in the history of the people of God. He drew closer in his relationship to his people to reveal the law, by which they were to live the faith, and not as something only to be read, studied or identified with. The law was to be lived. This continues into the New Testament when Our Lord Jesus Christ became flesh Himself, as this was the embodiment of the tablets of stone. The Word of God had actually become flesh in a human being, who is the living example of that written law — a law no longer just written, but enacted in every deed of the perfect human, the God-man, Jesus.

The stories provided serve as a very serious lesson for us in our modern approach to faith; we must not simply treat our homilies, catechetical talks, spiritual direction, or even this book, as a simple revelation from Mount Sinai, and then leave the law written on tablets of stone, without applying it practically to our personal lives. This would be contrary to the mission of Our Lord, the law made flesh. Rather, this book will help you take action in the most vital areas of your everyday life — actions that I believe are essential for every Catholic living in our fast-paced and constantly advancing modern world, filled with spiritual ambiguity and confusion. Furthermore, this book will not provide merely vague directional guidelines but will provide the 'how to' elements of the faith.

Our direct and vital mission as the faithful of the Church is to learn the law, as given on Mount Sinai by the prophet Moses, and take action with that law in our personal lives in a practical manner. Our Lord was very practical, as He was professionally a carpenter who knew his earthly trade well and would have shaped his human character to value clarity and taking precise action. This is why, as you read this book, you will undoubtedly make practical resolutions from your reflections upon the Word of God. The truth is meant to be listened to, and in doing so you will naturally enable the Word of God to become flesh in your personal life, even if just momentarily. The three practical 'tools' or 'tips' provided here are in the spirit of keeping your resolutions few and concise. I am a firm believer that when you make too many elaborate resolutions within a set timeframe, you are less likely to achieve them. Rather, keeping the focus to three resolutions is both trinitarian and short enough to attract our minds to start and finish these tasks well.

The enemy of our souls is likewise working through his spiritual and earthly agents to strategise for the destruction of members of Our Lord's body and the demise of their salvation. The forces of evil, through the mainstream media, pop culture, politics and in the everyday discourse of secularism, have not wasted any time in our modern age in plotting the demise of the holy Church. Let us talk specifically about the most recent times in the millennial age. Those same forces of evil have understood the mission by which they live. They have closed their minds, lips and hearts against the truth of God, and have practically plotted the persecution of the Church and the propagation of social evils. The real damage in all of this is that for the past five decades the people of God have not detected that a battle has been and continues to be waged and, most especially, have not been strategising for a battle against evil.

I hope you are able to see the clear parallels in the overall mission of my ministry, *The Catholic Toolbox*. I am on the frontlines of engaging myself and the faithful to learn, and quickly thereafter to plan practical solutions, to live the Catholic faith in our modern world.

You may be wondering, what does 'living the faith' actually entail? At the heart of living the faith is the daily pursuit of holiness, which, at some point, requires the introduction of a daily spiritual plan of attack. Such a plan allows you to sanctify yourself first, and then proceed to evangelise others effectively in your workplace, leisure activities, political endeavours and other social engagements. In doing so, you would have practical strategies on hand which you can implement to start these conversations, with the balancing touch of friendliness and engagement. Your strategy must be effective enough that it is reasonable to take action according to it, just like a magnetic pull with an urging force, which is the work of the Holy Spirit.

Furthermore, to live the Word of God in your own pursuit of salvation and sanctification, thereby resulting in the evangelisation of others, is the question of strategising for pastoral effectiveness. This subject is the means by which you are able to help others grow in holiness within the Church, and shine the light of Christ on a darkened world, in order for souls to dock at the port of Holy Mother Church. This deals with the question of our competition for Catholic social influence to be restored. Our influence is only to lead people to Christ for the salvation of souls and further sanctification or growth in holiness. This is why in these chapters you will discover topics which are very rarely discussed, such as 'Catholic Business Networking', enabling you to gain practical insights to return to your sphere of influence (or at least create one or more) and propagate the interests of the Church. Just like people in the world today have often been recruited and tasked with being agents of the evil one, we too must compensate for the years spent as an entire Church being intimidated and sidelined, to unveil, once again, a moral force within the world of the future.

The Faith in Our Coming Future

The years since the global financial crisis of 2008 have seen the world move at such a fast pace in all areas of technical and social development, accompanied by the effects of globalisation. As with then, we are now in the midst of another great crisis and economic depression, which comes at a time perhaps aligned with the outbreak of the latest coronavirus (COVID-19). The question most relevant to us now as Easter people is how will we utilise this once-in-a-lifetime opportunity in order to once again have the interests and mission of the Church spread to all the nations more effectively? Every crisis in Church history has given the people of God an opportunity to capitalise on the social condition of the time, to awaken humanity to the truths and realities of the world, thereby allowing the influence of the Church to grow in society as a whole, in order to bring many more souls to salvation.

I truly believe that the writing of this book has been providential and sentimental to the time in which we are living and the future that lies ahead. I firmly believe there is a wave of opportunity to once-again re-engage cradle Catholics who have lapsed from the faith, and those outside the Church, including the mainstream political and social spheres of influence. This is a time of crisis which can be best used to open people's eyes once again to the doctrinal and moral teachings of the Church, in order to help others discover that she is truly infallible. Moreover, we can awaken people to the countless examples of many saints and those in the making around us, which will then testify to the practicality or the liveability of the truth that His mystical body preaches.

Now let's touch on the importance of living examples of this mission we are on, to learn, strategise and implement the faith in our lives and the life of the Church, in order to draw more souls to Our Lord. It is crucial that we spend time in reflection on each chapter, in order to aspire to become a well-rounded Catholic, both spiritually and within our physical life in the community. I have carefully chosen crucial areas for reflection, that if mastered, will allow you to live an exponentially growing spiritual life. It is also crucial that we look at the lives of the saints of the past centuries for guidance, even if their insights and application of the Gospel may be distant to our experience as a Church in society today. It is helpful to consider both canonised saints in our more contemporary time, as well as those who I believe are good examples from our everyday life (saints in the making). By doing so, your mind will be trained for success, and will also be convinced that sometimes even the most difficult of moral teachings are not impossible to master. Your mentorship by great examples around you today can also become your quality assurance for the Church's teaching — that you are able to actually live the truths of the Gospel.

Through writing and speaking on my radio programs, presentations and consultations regarding these issues, I have grown in my conviction that a bright future and recovery of what I call the 'Catholic Market' is imminent; that the crisis in the Church today has been caused simply by a lack of action on the part of all the faithful. We are all equally to blame on a spiritual and practical level for our mistakes, but we will also be the first to learn from these evangelical failures of the past, and be able to fast-track over the coming years, after the pandemic is over, to a stronger position of Mass attendance and practice of the faith. This is not to mention the optimism I have regarding the possibility of mass conversions to the faith if we step out onto the scene again in public with confidence in our convictions.

This book would most certainly not have been possible without my creative director and co-founder of *The Catholic Toolbox* and *The Rite of Manhood*, Akita Sanchez, and her overwhelming support in what I believe I am able to offer to the Church, and what value I can bring to the table of reform and growth with both my skills and experience. I would also like to thank my parents and spiritual directors for their guidance over this past decade, to help me to grow in my resolve to both plan and work for reform, with the ultimate goal of seeing a healthy return of the faithful to

Rome in my lifetime. Furthermore, my greatest appreciation goes to all the clergy and lay faithful who have guided me on this journey of faith, who have demonstrated the very art of practical Catholicism in their lives. Your example has been the very guiding factor for my determination to help others to both repent and live a life of faith, and to believe that it can still be done in the difficult secular world of today.

This book has been carefully composed, compiling the experience and spiritual measures from everyday people, spiritual directors, and of the struggling faithful in our modern and ever-changing world. The purpose of this book is to aid the faithful to take practical measures to live the faith, which in turn will aid you in achieving your personal salvation and that of those around you.

Therefore, let this be your practical guide, which you can take into your everyday life in and outside the life of the Church, to help you implement your faith in our modern world. As the environment is changing rapidly and technology is updated, we too will need to update our practical strategies and customise our approach to living the faith today, without compromising a fraction of its essence. Let this be your guide through the upheaval we have incurred and for the storm ahead, so that we may ultimately become an *'Alter Christus'* or 'another Christ'.

Chapter I

Having the Grace to Start

When the saints lived the faith, the ultimate struggle for them was not spending vast amounts of time in accepting different Church teachings, unlike our sceptical world of today. Rather, the main focus was on perfecting the art of living it every day. Likewise, a return to the general acceptance of the teachings of holy mother Church is ideal, and what must also proceed is a great focus on taking action with that very same faith that was learnt and understood at the point of catechesis.

As James 1:22-23 very clearly exhorts us:

> *Be doers of the word, and not hearers only, deceiving yourselves. For if anyone is a hearer of the word and not a doer, he is like a man who observes his natural face in a mirror.*

What a radical idea, that we deceive ourselves by just treating the Word of God through the Church's teaching as a theory and failing to apply it to our lives. Your life of faith pertaining to your belief relies upon your response in taking action, and in turn — since we are not made for ourselves — the people around you who are relying on you for evangelisation. There is so much in the world that relies on each individual person growing in faith and having the courage to bear witness to the Gospel.

So, in embarking on this journey of mastering the art of practical Catholicism, in amending or simply enhancing the different areas of your faith, take heed of the three foundational tools before you set foot on this journey:

1. Pray and fast before starting this journey of transformation. You will need spiritual nourishment. This is an entire attitude and mindset change, that you strive to constantly live and implement the faith at every moment of your day in the midst of any circumstance. Praying about the start of this journey will aid you in actually being guided into God's will in living the faith wholeheartedly. This is a radical approach to the Gospel that also requires fasting. The significance of fasting is that it will provide mortification to both purify your resolve and reduce temptation of the flesh, which I believe is one of the greatest obstacles to growing in your relationship with your Creator.

2. Find a mentor to help you and keep you accountable. This can be a friend or, preferably, a family member, apart from your spiritual director. It's vital to be kept accountable from time to time by someone who you are close with on a personal level and who can see you often, without the boundary of being a spiritual director. They will also echo the struggle and hardships (you can count on the hardships to come). This is a mentor who can compare notes with you on ways to be effective in the world in living your faith and on what to look out for.

3. Reflect, for 10 minutes a day, on what your progress will look like, perhaps compared to the example of someone who you admire. Our expectations often get out of hand when we assume we are able to make massive changes to each area of our lives very quickly; we must allow for organic growth, and not see short-term zealousness as true progress. Take your time and don't expect instant results — the struggle and effort are the start of progress in the eyes of God. Often, we can be extremely harsh on ourselves because we are not immediately exceptional, and yet again this would be relative to one's point of view. The key is to remember that God is constantly proud of the struggle against sin, temptation or any failure to take action. Most especially in your reflection, meditate on the fact that complacency and simply throwing in the towel is the true disappointment. Remember always that it is the pressure that transforms coal into diamond.

Chapter 2

Focusing on achieving salvation

By this time in the book, we are actually getting to the point of why we are making all this effort in the first place. The sole reason we are seeking to apply Church teaching and to live it in our world today is to become like the Word made flesh Himself, Our Lord, and ultimately reach his kingdom in heaven. We can often get too distracted around the parish and diocesan life by administrative tasks, feast day celebrations, prayer groups, and youth activities to actually stop and reflect on what this is all actually for.

You may have heard it said: *'Extra Ecclesiam nulla salus'* or 'Outside the Church there is no salvation'. This statement finds its origins in St Cyprian of Carthage in the year 258 AD in his *Letter LXXII*. The purpose of this section is not to convince you that Our Lord and His Church are the only way to salvation, as this has been established for many years starting from His very words in John 14:6: *Jesus said to him, 'I am the way, and the truth, and the life; no one comes to the father, but by me'*. Rather, the challenge is: how do we personally embrace this ourselves? And if you are not convinced, let your action educate your mind on this subject.

The way in which we are able to practically apply this teaching directly to our lives is by using the following tools, which will keep our minds and hearts focused on the last and final judgement and on achieving the salvation of our souls:

1. What I like to call the morning and evening wake-up call. We all need a wake-up call, and an evening wake-up prompts you to reflect on the start and close of your day. You may also ponder whether all the work to be done has been accomplished and if it has been united with Christ for the salvation of your soul. It may seem fairly simple but, if implemented correctly, you will see some serious results.

2. Fortnightly confession. We all see that same person in the confession line every week after Mass — or it could even be ourselves, for that matter. Confession is the means by which we access the forgiveness of Christ, so having a healthy balance of frequenting it every second week is essential for remaining in the state of grace.

3. Nightly examination of conscience. Five minutes before we sleep is a useful time to remind ourselves of any deeds or guilt we may have accumulated throughout the day. Systematically run through each of the 10 commandments and look at each aspect of how you have lived your day, not just with respect to violating the law of God, but also with respect to the temptations you have had during the day to act against these, as a potential symptom of a pending sin. If you do this every night, you will be on a good path back to your next scheduled confession, and will shorten it significantly.

Chapter 3

Living your liturgy

The Mass being the re-presentation of the sacrifice on Calvary, the source and summit of our faith from which all the activity of the Church derives and flows, is the centre of our faith. It is vital to understand that the Mass does not exist for our own personal satisfaction, or to cater to our emotional or personal needs. It is there as an act of worship to almighty God. However, the added beauty of the Mass, in all rites and forms in which it exists today, assists us in directing all our senses to the divine work of God in the liturgy. It is the sound of chant, incense, bells, and even the architectural beauty, organically developed over centuries, that clothes the Mass with these external beauties, ensuring our minds and hearts in the true spirit of 'worship' are able to conform ourselves to the unseen spiritual realities taking place.

According to *The Constitution on the Sacred Liturgy* of Vatican II, paragraph 43:

> *At the Last Supper, on the night He was betrayed, our Savior instituted the eucharistic sacrifice of His Body and Blood. This He did in order to perpetuate the sacrifice of the Cross through the ages until He should come again, and so to entrust to His beloved Spouse, the Church, a memorial of His death and resurrection: a sacrament of love, a sign of unity, a bond of charity, a paschal banquet in which Christ is consumed, the mind is filled with grace, and a pledge of future glory is given to us.*

His sacrament of love is also within the context of the heavenly worship which we engage at the holy Mass, along with all the angels and saints participating with us and even the souls in purgatory. The Mass has a cosmological nature essentially, and once someone discovers this, coupled with the fact that the bread and wine turn into Christ's Body and Blood, we can't turn back. When we understand this reality, every other aspect of our prayer life will make sense. Deriving from the Eucharistic sacrifice is also the Liturgy of the Hours, or Divine Office (that I highly recommend you pray with a breviary or even your smartphone). This form of prayer is second to the holy Mass and would be beneficial for our spiritual lives to aid in providing structure to it.

Here are three practical tips in order to live your liturgy authentically in your everyday spiritual life, and to be an example of someone who is a living liturgy themselves:

1. Write down a handful of extracts from the Mass which can be prayed and applied at work, within the home and during your leisure time. For instance, when I wash my hands, I pray the prayer found in the 'lavabo' (washing of the hands of a priest). The effectiveness of sometimes carrying out a peculiar habit can draw your daily connection back to the source and summit of our faith.

2. Before each Mass, spend 10 to 15 minutes reflecting on the realities that are about to take place; this can act as a warm-up for your attendance to the worship of God. For about five minutes after Mass it would also be necessary to reflect on the realities that took place, and to make a thanksgiving. This is basically your chance to digest the spiritual phenomenon that occurred, to assist you in your progress and appreciation of this very sacrament, which we should never take for granted in any place, time or season.

3. The best way to live the Mass is to attend it more often than the Sunday obligation. Though I will not provide you with a precise guideline, it helps to know that each saint understood that they needed the Mass daily to see spiritual progress. Much like how people work out five times per week to see results, start by adding one additional Mass a week apart from Sunday and then increase the frequency every two months, until you can finally achieve daily Mass. The struggle here is that you do not want to become complacent in your attendance, lest it becomes another daily habit or ritual with no living purpose on a personal level. This is absolutely crucial when you are assessing your spiritual growth, which is why the first two tips mentioned above are so vital in keeping a genuine spirit of participation in this mystery of our faith.

Chapter 4

How to evangelise in your workplace

This is by far one of the hardest tasks you must consistently master as a member of the body of Christ. There in the midst of your ordinary circumstances, you must find God and spread the Gospel to your colleagues. This can be tricky. The problem is, when we bring up religion, it can become a touchy subject that is often avoided at all costs. It causes controversies and divisions, and it rightfully should, even at the expectation of Our Lord, so radically that he said in Matthew 10:34-35:

> *Do not think that I have come to bring peace on the earth; I have not come to bring peace, but a sword. For I have come to set a man against his father, and a daughter against her mother, and a daughter-in-law against her mother-in-law.*

The words of Our Lord are applicable to the context of the professional workplace today, where disagreements are seen to be something that causes hatred and division, rather than a good intellectual balance and a challenge for each other. This is why most Catholics struggle to be effective in this area: it can either cost them the business they are trying to draw, their high-paying job or, most detrimental, can give them the reputation as 'the religious person' in the office. It is a legitimate struggle for the professionals who want to heed the call of Our Lord to 'make disciples of all nations, baptising them in the name of the Father and of the Son and of the Holy Spirit' (Matthew 28:19). As with every challenge that has arisen in Church history, it is not impossible to re-evangelise professionally and within the relevant social setting. The three practical tactics I am about to share with you have personally worked for me and hundreds of other faithful:

1. Build your respect and reputation around your workplace or business, by growing professionally exceptional in your work. There is nothing worse than for you to be carrying out poor quality work and then reveal that you are a practising Catholic, when the Church's reputation is not currently in its prime. Find a career mentor in your field, possibly one of faith, and allow them to guide you to improve or even better your work. I recommend that your mentor should be someone who possibly even works within your field or sector, to give you an insight into the culture found within that particular career. Every workplace evangelisation strategy requires that customised approach to the culture and the specific people within your organisation. What I am essentially suggesting is that you draft a systematic plan to mention your faith and find a point of target for sharing the Gospel with each individual member in your direct workplace domain. This may sound peculiar, but, in reality given the climate of hostility towards religion altogether, you need to be a cunning snake in your tactical approach to shining the light of Christ.

2. Start with what I call the 'Weekend Evangelise Method' (WEM). Speaking from personal experience, this is the easiest time to reveal your faith, after having established your reputation and grounding in a workplace. When someone asks how the weekend was, mention your usual chronological events and conclude with having attended Mass, and constantly bring up church events within this context. If you have a non-western cultural heritage, you could possibly use this as a way to mention your faith. For instance, if you are a Croatian Catholic, you could possibly start by talking about a cultural event which was incorporated by your church, since faith and culture can be inextricable.

3. The 'Personal Evangelisation Method' (PEM). That is, utilise events away from the workplace or even during travel time in a car and apply the weekend method above to connect with individual colleagues. Then, you can proceed to ask them questions about the journey of faith or spiritual life they are on. You will observe how your colleagues will open up when away from the desk or workplace. This is a specific approach that has worked marvels in many scenarios through the workplaces and experiences of numerous professionals. Individually having these conversations with each member of your immediate staff will build the foundation to talk about faith with all staff members collectively, as they will all have insight into your spiritual and moral voice.

Chapter 5

How to defend your faith in any context

The art of apologetics is a branch of evangelisation itself. It is a speciality in defending and explaining the faith and not apologising — 'Sorry for being Catholic.' It derives its name from the Greek term *'apologia'* meaning 'defence' or 'answer', used in 1 Peter 3:15: *'But in your hearts reverence Christ as Lord. Always be prepared to make a defence to anyone who calls you to account for the hope that is in you, yet do it with gentleness and reverence'*.

Consider the following scenario: You find yourself at a dinner party, and the conversations are running smoothly, until Uncle Bob, who left the faith 15 years ago, begins to comment about how the Church is out-of-date and should 'get with the times'. What you need to be able to do is to raise your glass with charm, explain reasonably and eloquently why you believe in what he militantly opposes, and impress him, along with his like-minded crowd around you, with your classy and knowledgeable comeback. I can personally describe the effectiveness of doing so in social settings, or anywhere for that matter; you will be able to leave with a feeling of accomplishment carried out by the Holy Spirit.

Let us break down the methodology for how to defend your faith in any social setting you find yourself in today, based on what St Peter sets as the standard. There are three practical ways to go about this:

1. Sanctification is the key to being able to have the mindset and grace to defend the faith. Praying and living the faith as your sanctification is the prerequisite for being able to explain it from the heart and not as a mere textbook theory. Check your prayer life, and make sure that what you are about to explain isn't contrary to what you are living, which they may later see as a colleague, family member or friend especially. Otherwise, state clearly that you may have a struggle with a habit or have previously done wrong, and that you are aspiring to be better, as your human frailty should not stop you from your duty to evangelise in this case. If we all waited to become perfect before evangelising, this would be a problem.

2. State the answer clearly, and ask for feedback from your opponent. In the case that you find yourself not having an adequate response — or any response, for that matter — tell them that you don't know (displaying humility) and that you will return with an answer for the questions that they have. Seek an answer from an approved Church organisation or a source of Church teaching that possibly contains an imprimatur or nihil obstat, meaning the source has been verified to be in accordance with the Magisterium or teaching authority of the Church and is free from heresy.

3. Exercise respect and charm. This is simply where your social and charm skills come to hand. You can be a

prayerful soul and theologian at the same time, but if you cannot communicate clearly and respectfully you will not engage the opponent sufficiently. The key to doing this is to keep your calm (or at least fake it till you make it), as this will impress upon them that you have confidence. Include some humour during the conversation and conclude on a high note.

Chapter 6

Sanctification of everyday work

To become a well-rounded person in your faith, you must proceed now to a more advanced but necessary stage of using the conscience of God around you in the world, bringing Him into the ordinary circumstances of your daily life.

In our modern age we have seen the example of St Josemaría Escrivá. In *Conversations*, number 70, he speaks about the vocation to take God into ordinary life:

> *The vocation to Opus Dei confirms all this: to such an extent that one of the essential signs of this vocation is precisely a determination to remain in the world and to do a job as perfectly as possible (taking into account, of course, one's personal imperfections), both from the human and from the supernatural point of view. This means it must be a job which contributes effectively towards both the building up of the earthly city — and therefore it must be done competently and*

> *in a spirit of service; and to the consecration of the world — and in this regard it must both sanctify and be sanctified.*

He then proceeds to elaborate on the importance of connecting one's self with the workmanship of Our Lord in His time as a carpenter. It is a truly unique analysis of this aspect of his 33 years, of which not much was written. Our Lord can provide us with an example of professionalism in our work as continued below:

> *Those who want to live their faith perfectly and to do apostolate according to the spirit of Opus Dei, must sanctify themselves with their work, must sanctify their work and sanctify others through their work. It is while they work alongside their equals, their fellow working men from whom they are in no way different, they strive to identify themselves with Christ, imitating His thirty years in the workshop in Nazareth.*

There are three practical ways in which we can sanctify our time at work, so that we do not compartmentalise God in just our church and prayer time:

1. Set hourly to bi-hourly reminders on your phone or by memory, in order to make a thanksgiving for this time undertaken in work. Also, quickly review how efficiently and well you have used this time.

2. Offer up this break for prayer intentions, which could be for the Pope, a Bishop or a friend. Remember that one hour of work is one hour of prayer, especially as the Benedictine protocol states, 'Ora et labora', that is, to work and pray. However, in the context of your everyday life, your work becomes your prayer, if it is sanctified.

3. Place a small image on your workstation, no matter

where this is, and look at it several times through each hour, whenever you get a chance. This will also act as an effortless evangelisation tool.

Chapter 7

Living as an Easter people

Now let's talk about the end of time. This is one of the most confused and anticipated events of human history to come. To become a well-rounded Catholic it is necessary to monitor your life of faith, not worrying about any end times at all. However, when Our Lord says in Matthew 24:43-44:

> *But know this, that if the householder had known in what part of the night the thief was coming, he would have watched and would not have let his house be broken into. Therefore you also must be ready; for the son of man is coming at an hour you do not expect.*

You should have some sort of anticipation, although it is not something to stress about. This may affect your future on earth, if He does return in your time, or in heaven when we will return back to our bodies (age or looks yet to be determined, but hopefully to our younger and more attractive selves). Our Lord's return to earth should not distract us from the main mission at hand, which is to work for the salvation of our soul, and henceforth grow in holiness. An overemphasis on apocalyptic events and preparing for the end times in an obsessive sense is unhealthy for the life of a Catholic. Our Lord, coming like a thief in the night, should find us doing our usual business of living our faith every day. The main objective of this life is to get to heaven, regardless of the second coming, so that when He does return, you may find yourself on the side of the sheep (Matthew 25:31-46) returning back to your body and living in the new and improved heaven and earth to come.

In order to avoid the traps of obsession, and to authentically prepare for Our Lord's second coming (with the time remaining being none of our business) the following practical tips will hopefully help you to find yourself at peace and in a good place:

1. Bi-monthly adoration visits of 30 minutes to one hour, in order to visualise the start of your adoration as Christ's second coming. If you are close with Our Lord and have a strong personal relationship, then, whether you are at adoration or not and He comes an hour later, it's the same Lord and the same conversation that must continue.

2. Visit a cemetery or graveyard biannually. This will help to keep you in check regarding the reality of death and, more excitingly, our return to our bodies once Our Lord comes again. You could choose to visit on All Souls Day (and even gain a full or partial indulgence on the day) and/or on the death anniversary of a loved one.

3. Detach from the mainstream media's portrayal of real-world events that could be perceived as apocalyptic, and find the facts through your own research. This will allow you to keep a steady and healthy eye on the events unfolding as possible indications of when

Christ will return. We know for a fact the time is only getting closer, but we will never know the actual day. So, understanding yourself and contrasting with other human events could assist you in praying for what is happening, and asking Christ to delay His coming so that he may find a Church and humanity worthier of His kingdom when He arrives.

Chapter 8

How to incorporate mary into your spiritual life

Mary can be a difficult yet simple person to incorporate into one's spiritual life, especially given that our worship alone belongs to the Blessed Trinity. The reason that I say this is because she can sometimes be perceived to have been elevated to the level of Our Lord. The balance and health equilibrium regarding Mary needs to be mastered very seriously to both avoid neglecting Our Lady as a very powerful mother and intercessor, while still understanding that she was a creature and we do not owe any kind of worship to her.

The reason behind this is that during my Protestant-minded years I began to neglect Mary, after witnessing many times my grandmother and other pious older men and women pray to her almost excessively. However, I later realised that regardless of the actions or lack of intentions of other individuals, Church teaching still stands and the fact remains that she is our mother and she ought to be only venerated as our mother and as a prime example of a Christian.

Mary is most elevated in scripture during her Assumption and Coronation which is indicated in Revelation 12:1-4:

> *And a great sign appeared in heaven, a woman clothed with the sun, with the moon under her feet, and on her head a crown of twelve stars; she was with a child and she cried out in her pangs of birth, in anguish for delivery. And another sign appeared in heaven; behold, a great red dragon, with seven heads and ten horns, and seven diadems upon his heads. His tail swept down a third of the stars of heaven, and cast them to the earth. And the dragon stood before the woman who was about to bear a child, that he might devour the child when she brought it forth.*

1. Pray the rosary daily. If you are struggling to do so or complete the entire rosary, take my 'RRP challenge': the Rosary Rehabilitation Program entails a five-week challenge. In the first week, complete one decade a day. In the second week, complete two decades a day, until the full rosary has been incorporated fully after the fifth week. This is a slow and healthy transition over a five-week period, which can assist us in an authentic appreciation of this devotion.

2. Buy an image of Christ and place or hang the image within a designated prayer space. Later, add an image of Our Lady to the left of Christ. This will allow you to mentally visualise the hierarchy in heaven — that Mary, our mother, is an intercessor and an assistant to direct us to her Son alone.

3. Mental prayer directed towards Mary. The best way to appreciate Our Blessed Mother is to actually speak with her personally, in a session of mental prayer. This could be a couple of minutes of your mental prayer with the Blessed Trinity; we can then start a side or

full conversation for several minutes with her to train ourselves that she is part of our mission of salvation. She is indeed the first true example of a human who lived holiness like us, as she was not truly God. Take that fact right there into your reflection and personal discussion with Our Lady.

Chapter 9

Fighting daily spiritual warfare

'*We belong to the Church Militant; and she is militant because on earth the powers of darkness are ever restless to encompass her destruction,*' (Venerable Pope Pius XII in *Discorso Di Sua Santita*, 1953).

The concept of the 'Church Militant' or *Ecclesia Militans* became prevalent during a time when a major world war was underway. This then brought the attention of the Catholic world and others to the reality that we are indeed militant in our faith on a daily basis. This is because there is a serious war being waged by the devil and his fellow demons from hell against every human being at every moment of the day, especially as you read this. Hell indeed is not rejoicing as you read this battle instruction material against its forces.

We must reflect and understand that there is a battle for our souls every single day, in order to have us commit and live a consistent life of sin, thereby becoming instruments of evil. Now this, by far, is the easiest route that every human being can take; you have a serious choice if you would like to challenge yourself and fight this tide working against you, not out of simple opposition but out of love for God only. We are called not to take the route of comfort and let the tide drift us but rather to grow in strength (through prayer and penance) in order to have the fortitude to paddle against the tide of sin.

Spiritual warfare on heresy within the Church

It is in the midst of analysing spiritual warfare as a whole that we come to understand that, in fact, the greatest enemy of the Church is not outside the walls of her fortress but within. This is perfectly exemplified in the betrayal of Our Lord Jesus Christ by Judas Iscariot in Matthew 26:14-16:

> *Then one of the twelve, who was called Judas Iscariot, went to the chief priests and said 'What will you give me if I deliver him to you?' And they paid him thirty pieces of silver. And from that moment he sought an opportunity to betray him.*

If we clearly observe the systematic process of ecclesiastical betrayal (or in any other context for that matter), what we will find is that it begins with temptation. In the case of Judas, he was tempted to increase his wealth by thirty pieces of silver, thereby transpiring into the complete abuse of trust. Likewise, how often have many clergy and indeed laity betrayed Our Lord in this manner, where there is a temptation that blinds and dulls our conscience within that particular moment? Then we proceed to commit that sin or propagate that heresy, all for the glorification of our ego. There is a reason I believe that Judas himself was chosen as one of the apostles, and that is simply to play his part in demonstrating to the universal body of Christ that we are not immune from sin, even among the hierarchy. This is exemplified throughout the centuries where we have had numerous cases of infidelity by either not living the faith or propagating heresy.

Let us focus on heresy itself, and its implications for both the person and faithful who are thus deceived by such errors. Heresy is the direct opposite to the truth of the Gospel, as authorised by the Church.

In our modern world, especially within the Church's society, we are not exempt from being taken by the tide, let alone from acknowledging that there is a tide against us in the water. However, we need to encourage and remind each other, despite our state of life, that we must keep a firm eye on the true battle, where on the other side awaits our victory of salvation. In order to take action now in incorporating a spirit of militancy in our everyday Catholic life, adhere seriously to the following tools I have equipped you with, and you will have greater strength and the ability to carry on in your daily battle:

1. Invoke St Michael's prayer in the start and close of your day, and when you are feeling spiritually tempted by the devil. St Michael the Archangel will surely aid you, especially after Pope Leo XIII had a vision of hell and the devil himself. I also suggest a 10-minute reflection once a week on this prayer and the spiritual assistance it is able to provide us with as a people of God in our daily spiritual warfare. Furthermore, I suggest incorporating this prayer during the close of your morning and evening offering, and, for parish priests, during the recession of the holy Mass.

2. The use of sacramentals. This tool is strong, assuming that you are attending the sacraments and are in a regular routine of prayer. Furthermore, they are not magic charms that will perform miracles, but if your faith is strong, they will act to assist you, in a way that is directly proportional to the strength of your spiritual life. So, the power of possessing and placing a Benedictine medal (remember to have the priest administer the special blessing only) over your neck,

in your pocket or car will dispel demonic influence. Furthermore, the blessing of one's self with holy water and exorcised salt (consult your parish priest for this) will aid you in fighting spiritual temptation. These three sacramentals for you to take advantage of will undoubtedly be efficacious.

3. You must then devise a temptation attack plan. Temptation is a very interesting area to analyse. To explain in warfare terminology, it is an ambush, designed to inflict spiritual damage when we are off guard. This echoes the words of the Lord's Prayer: 'Lead us not into temptation'. In other words, it is inevitable in your life journey. This also acts as a great test of faith that you must live up to. This is what I like to implement as a three-second rule when tempted. When you find temptation to sin, count for three seconds and then start with St Michael's prayer, then proceed with two minutes of mental prayer. You will find that if this is executed correctly, it will be highly effective for you.

Chapter 10

Living your faith with good money

As someone who is fond of investing my money, I am very enthusiastic and motivated in this aspect of my life. That is why I needed to really reflect, study and ask questions — if prolonging and engaging in excessive money-making is something that might be too obsessive, and may hinder my spiritual life.

We can all feel a sense of guilt about our material achievements or aspirations when we hear the passage from the Gospel of Matthew 19:20-22:

> *The young man said to him, 'All these I have observed; what do I still lack?' Jesus said to him, 'If you would be perfect, go, sell what you possess and give to the poor, and you will have treasure in heaven; and come, follow me'. When the young man heard this he went away sorrowful; for he had great possessions.*

In a world dominated by socialist ideas about money, we

need to understand that Our Lord does not desire anyone to be poor or to have no money; nor to become wealthy. Money and earthly wealth simply do not matter before the throne of God. Whether you are homeless, struggling to pay your electricity bill, financially well off, or are a millionaire, billionaire or trillionaire, the numbers mean nothing to Our Lord. If you are striving to live your faith and attain the salvation of your soul and you happen to be financially successful then you have an added benefit to your life in terms of comfort. What Our Lord is trying to say to the rich man in the Gospel is that the wealthy man is in fact being held back by his riches in his relationship with God. As long as we use our wealth to feed our families, build the Church, carry out our moral obligations, and not become attached to it, instead focussing our life on our salvation and relationship with God, then we are on the path to spiritual and financial success.

We have all met poor people who are greedy or obsessed with money more than the rich. The true test of character is if you lose all your wealth, because of an economic situation or due to an unfortunate occurrence, and your faith and hope in God remains the same and unchanged. This, I believe, is a vital litmus test for your attachment to earthly goods.

In order to take action now with this vital subject, and to remain strong in our faith and focus on God, we must sanctify our wealth and success for the glory of God. In the spirit of St Josemaría, as we previously discussed, take heed of the following practical tools:

1. Donate a fixed percentage of your income to the work of the Church through your parish or an independent ecclesiastically approved apostolate. You can verify this with your diocese, or cross-check that the apostolate is approved in some manner. The importance of contributing your hard-earned time or money, which are both of monetary value, is that the

investment may be able to assist the work of God to advance through the chosen organisation.

2. Spend a few minutes before you start your daily professional task asking God for the grace not to labour in vain, and reflect on the 'why' of your work. It may be for your family or for others that you work; think of your next pay cheque as your living expense and an opportunity to help you grow closer to Our Lord.

3. Pray while you work, so that while you work, aspects of your spiritual and financial life are growing. For an in-depth explanation, refer back to Chapter 6. As the old Benedictine phrase says: 'Ora et labora', that is, 'to work and pray'. This was a great monastic concept that guided both eastern and western Christianity, and should be applied to our everyday lives.

Chapter II

Passing on the Faith to the Next Generation

In our time, we are experiencing a serious divide between how our parents, grandparents and the preceding generations passed on the faith and our modern situation. As the old saying says, 'You cannot give what you do not have'. I believe this explains the underlying problem of why less than or just greater than 10 percent of Catholics attend Mass, of whom many still have not had the opportunity to experience the fullness of the faith. We have found ourselves in this situation due to those who no longer believe or who have abandoned the faith altogether for the past four decades. Hopefully, we are able to fast-track the revitalisation of the Church's catechesis, especially with such a fast-paced and pleasure-seeking world today, as we may not know the extent to which we can recover the faithful and the newer generations to come.

Let us reflect on the words of Our Lord Himself in Matthew 18:5-7 when he speaks about leading the young ones astray, which perhaps we may have been guilty of by not educating them about the faith:

> *Whoever receives one such child in my name receives me; but whoever causes one of these little ones who believe in me to sin, it would be better for him to have a great millstone fastened round his neck and to be drowned in the depth of the sea. Woe to the world for temptations to sin! For it is necessary that temptations come, but woe to the man by whom the temptation comes!*

It is not a time to despair but rather to focus on a more effective strategy for the next five-to-ten-year period, effective immediately. What I am about to elaborate on in the three practical tools for this chapter will assist you in your sphere of influence to take action and to assist Catholic education for our youth, so that we may allow them to grow and remain in the faith:

1. Get a hold of the Catechism of the Catholic Church and other relevant Church-approved material to teach the young within your spheres of influence. Within your family, youth group or even in class if you are a teacher, begin to introduce Church teaching through these means. Refer to the end of this book for some recommendations for material and media outlets that could assist you if you do not yet have the confidence to teach the faith yourself.

2. Write a letter and meet with your Bishop. I cannot stress how important this is and how much of a difference it can make when a Bishop sees and hears from the everyday faithful concerned about the future of our children's catechesis in opposition to the influence of the modern world. Bishops are the shepherds of the flock of Christ, which he has subdivided into differing lots.

   Therefore, we are the local sheep in our diocese and must be active in the work of our shepherd, for sometimes sheep can alert their shepherd that there is danger or that something needs addressing. There is no point in entertaining complacency as laity, believing that our voice would never be heard nor have a significant impact on the hierarchy. The performance of a Bishop is only as good as the clergy and laity around him, both professionally and among the faithful. Therefore, I urge you to constantly be in regular contact with your bishop and his staff to voice your concerns.

3. Write and speak to your parish priest or other officials in your ecclesiastical organisation. The Bishop may be the head of the diocese, but all changes will inevitably be made on a local level and compounded over the diocese as a whole. You need to make sure your voice is heard and your influence is made in this sphere. Perhaps start a parish or organisation formation program catering to youth and young adults.

Furthermore, it is imperative to foster strong relationships with the parish council, whether you are a member or not, since there can be great dialogue on this pastoral level. The Bishop in each diocese is definitely accessible to every one of his flock, however, there can be more open and frequent discussions with your parish priest. Also, you will most often see immediate implementations of your ideas since a parish is much smaller in size in comparison with a diocese. Your relationship with and zeal towards your local parish priest is of the utmost importance if you ever plan being effective in your ministry.

Chapter 12

How to support and encourage your bishop

We just spoke about supporting and encouraging your Bishop for the education of the young in the Church today. Let's now focus on your influence with your Bishop as a priest or as an ordinary member of the diocese. It is vital that sometimes the Bishop's flock alerts or awakens the Bishop to take action in any area of the faith that needs to be attended to. From a young age, in high school, I never had any obstacles in both contacting my Bishop and making sure my voice was readily heard. At one stage I was described as a modern crusader for the faith! This was a flattering statement at the time, in 2010. However, this is a clear message to everyone reading this book: no age is ever too young to have your voice heard by the Bishop, diocese or even by the Pope himself. Keep your mindset strong, aim to have your voice heard and persist incessantly until you have been given a response.

According to the Dogmatic Constitution on the Church, *Lumen Gentium*, paragraph 10:

> *Though they differ from one another in essence and not only in degree, the common priesthood of the faithful and the ministerial or hierarchical priesthood are nonetheless interrelated: each of them in its own special way is a participation in the one priesthood of Christ. The ministerial priest, by the sacred power he enjoys, teaches and rules the priestly people; acting in the person of Christ, he makes present the Eucharistic sacrifice, and offers it to God in the name of all the people. But the faithful, in virtue of their royal priesthood, join in the offering of the Eucharist. They likewise exercise that priesthood in receiving the sacraments, in prayer and thanksgiving, in the witness of a holy life, and by self-denial and active charity.*

Furthermore in the application of this, it is also worth noting the following assertion from Canon 212 of the Code of Canon Law:

> *§2. The Christian faithful are free to make known to the pastors of the Church their needs, especially spiritual ones, and their desires.*

> *§3. According to the knowledge, competence, and prestige which they possess, they have the right and even at times the duty to manifest to the sacred pastors their opinion on matters which pertain to the good of the Church and to make their opinion known to the rest of the Christian faithful, without prejudice to the integrity of faith and morals, with reverence toward their pastors, and attentive to common advantage and the dignity of persons.*

I would like to elaborate on the aspect of the common priesthood of all believers, as priest, prophet and king. We the laity have the duty to unite ourselves, not in the same Apostolic way as an ordained priest, but rather in a general, common manner by virtue of our baptism. As prophets, we have the duty to teach, and this can be a good lesson for our shepherds that they listen and learn from the faithful who have strong insights about the world in which they live. Therefore, take heed and action with the following practical tools to engage and encourage your Bishop:

1. Write a letter of concern addressing any issue to the Bishop. Also address and send separate copies to the relevant vicar general/s within your diocese. Often the people surrounding the Bishop are those who take administrative control, and to effectively get your point across, you must also follow up with a phone call or even a visit to the desk. Having something in writing in dealing with the corporate side of the Church is an essential place to start.

2. Book a physical meeting with the Bishop or vicar general/s, and take a physical copy of your letter, points of concerns, and set a timeframe of accountability. This assists in following up the points that have been raised and discussed to track any progress on the diocesan end. What you must always consider and understand in your dealings with diocesan staff is that they are also addressing the concerns of your entire local Church boundary, and so friendly reminders and regular follow ups with the personal assistants of your bishop or vicar general/s will allow any processes to move much more expediently.

3. Ask the important and even the serious and sometimes controversial questions when a Bishop is giving a public address, because they are physically present before you and will also be answering to all the faithful. What better way is there than to have your shepherd address the thoughts and minds of the many who may often need some light shone on a particular subject of administration or the faith? Make sure to

also see the Bishop personally about your concerns after the assembly.

Chapter 13

Overcoming sins of the flesh

Now we have arrived at one of the most challenging aspects that you will find in your lifetime as a member of the body of Christ. To overcome the sins of the flesh we must first start by reflecting on the subject of mortal sin as articulated in paragraph 1855 of the Catechism of the Catholic Church:

> *Mortal sin destroys charity in the heart of man by a grave violation of God's law; it turns man away from God, who is his ultimate end and his beatitude, by preferring an inferior good to him. Venial sin allows charity to subsist, even though it offends and wounds it.*

Mortal sins are what cause us to break away from our relationship with God, hence we then require spiritual resuscitation through the sacrament of confession. We must understand the gravity of sins of the flesh; for example, the sins related to our human sexuality and also situations of extreme gluttony. We as human beings have a natural, carnal desire for these sins, as these are embedded in our humanity, which makes this fight more difficult, but not impossible with the grace of God. To understand the gravity of the sins related to our human flesh, they are best summed up in the words of Our Lady (within the context of the approaching modern age): 'More souls go to hell because of sins of the flesh than for any other reason,' (The Message of Our Lady of Fatima [Selections], 1917).

Now if we will keep our passions and human carnal desires in check to avoid the inevitable consequences, we need to remember that Our Lord and Our Lady are on our side in this battle. So radically we must take advantage of the sacraments and graces in order to succeed in achieving a consistent level of sexual and other carnal stability within our flesh being directed by our soul. If we are going to succeed in this battle against the sins of the flesh, then we not only need to employ spiritual tactics but we also need to use practical strategies aligned with the flesh itself. This, I believe, has been the missing piece of the puzzle in many spiritual directions, talks, lectures and general advice. So, let's look at the three radically important practical tools to help you master this area of your life:

1. When temptation arises, snap into a mode of reflection for 15 minutes in order to understand where the origin of these thoughts or temptations are coming from. There must be an underlying factor for them, and you need to capture the essence of why you are being tempted in any area of your life.

2. Let's now talk about mortification. Methods of mortification can include fasting, cold showers (I highly recommend these for any sort of temptation) and denying yourself pleasures. This can be powerful, but the pendulum can swing the other way if you do not spend time at the end of the day reflecting on

the 'why' of each mortification undertaken. This is because of our human complacency if we do things blindly or become overzealous.

3. Reflect on your own death to come in moments of temptation. This can have a profound effect on your human psychology, in the sense that you do not want to be offending God with your mortal body, and also that the flesh and its temptations are always temporary. This will aid you in snapping out of the sins of the flesh and in holistically reflecting about your life in general, measured in years from birth to death. Try it and you will be very surprised.

Chapter 14

Traditional or Traditionalist?
Balancing Tradition Today

This brings me to one of my favourite topics over the years, which every Catholic will notice at some stage of their journey. Whether you are a cradle Catholic or a convert to the faith, the scenarios below may be something you have become familiar with. You may have accidentally stumbled into a church on the odd afternoon and may have seen the priest saying Mass in Latin with his back to the people (this practice is classified as *'ad orientem'* — which means 'to the east', which is the direction of the rising sun). As you have noticed, the majority of the debate around tradition revolves around the form of Mass.

You probably have asked yourself, 'Why did the Mass change so dramatically from what we now know as the Extraordinary Form of the Roman rite (Latin Mass) to the 'Novus Ordo' Mass of 1969, which is used in the average parish today?' The answer is not very simple, and would be the subject of another book one day perhaps; as a liturgical enthusiast myself, I cannot fully grasp the entirety of the underlying cause to be able to answer this question here.

The aim of this chapter is to provide you with the understanding that Tradition has both a 'big T' and 'little t', and that the fact remains that both forms of the Roman rite are fully valid and worthy of use. Often the radical traditionalists will spend time arguing with the progressives in the Church, not realising that, though most Catholics use the Latin rite as the liturgy, it is not the only form of Mass available. Let us not forget the other two dozen or so Eastern Catholic Rites that are also equally valid and worthy of our spiritual participation.

My personal view is that the Latin Mass does indeed contain some greater theological manifestations of the reality of the Eucharistic sacrifice. This is perhaps because the timeframe of the Council during the social upheaval caused some aspects of the rite to be removed, for reasons that are still debatable.

Radical traditionalism, which is exemplified in the rebellious activity of the Society of St Pius X and juxtaposed alongside the radical desacralisation of the Mass through liturgical chaos and modernism, are both examples of the extreme ends of the pendulum. The correct approach to this situation was single-handedly demonstrated by Pope Emeritus Benedict XVI in his *Motu Proprio, Summorum Pontificum*, in 2007. This document liberated the Latin Mass further from the provisions of Pope John Paul II, to further allow any priest of the Roman rite to celebrate the Mass of 1962 without the permission of the Bishop. In doing so, he stated the following in article 1:

> *The Roman Missal promulgated by Pope Paul VI is the ordinary expression of the* lex orandi *(rule of prayer) of the Catholic Church of the Latin rite. The Roman Missal promulgated by Saint Pope Pius V and revised by Blessed Pope John XXIII is nonetheless to be considered*

> *an extraordinary expression of the same* lex orandi *of the Church and duly honoured for its venerable and ancient usage. These two expressions of the Church's* lex orandi *will in no way lead to a division in the Church's* lex credendi *(rule of faith); for they are two usages of the one Roman rite.*

What is vital to understand is that both forms of the same rite as described above are not opposed to each other, though we may notice differences in each one. The questionable changes in the 1969 Mass could even be further improved through exposure to the 1962 Mass. So, a healthy balance of both is the ultimate solution to any progress in the future. We must not allow prolonged obsession with the Roman liturgical forms to create division and hence compromise the objective work of the Church, for the salvation of souls.

So how are you to make sense of this tradition dilemma and find a healthy balance as a Catholic? You may have already experienced this in the Church or will inevitably encounter this situation in the future. Make very serious note of what I am about to advise you with the following three practical tips:

1. Let's start by putting the Roman liturgy aside. Let us venture east, to experience all the eastern rites (fulfilling your Sunday obligation) within your city; for example, the Maronite, Syrian, Chaldean, Syro-Malabar, Syro-Malankara, Byzantine (Family of Churches), Coptic, Ethiopian and Armenian rites. Systematically take the one-year challenge of attending every single one of the above in your city and you will have shaped your liturgical experience. This eliminates excessive centralisation on the Roman rite and will help you become liturgically holistic. Also, it will be a cool thing to tell both your traditional and charismatic friends!

2. Attend the traditional Latin Mass and the Novus Ordo between two weeks of each other and document both similarities and differences, then seek the relevant answers from a credible source — most especially from the clergy with whom you attended these liturgies. The importance of this is to ensure that you have a harmonious understanding of the origins of the new rite of Mass today, from the ancient rite from which it developed. The traditional Mass essentially is your background information for the Ordinary Form.

3. Find ways as a server, liturgist, lay person or in whatever capacity you find yourself in, to refer and help others experience the Latin Mass as a new and spiritually-enriching experience. This is so they too can become enriched by both forms of the Mass. Consider asking your parish priest to start the Latin Mass in your parish. Ask a priest who understands the Latin Mass to give a catechesis, or run a discussion in a group you may be part of.

Chapter 15

How to pray consistently

When you are at the level of taking your faith seriously and living it as Our Lord commanded, you must fight the habit of sloth and complacency, which are heavily prevalent in our modern world. Sometimes we can find ourselves overzealous and aspiring to attain the spiritual level of mysticism as found in the lives of the desert fathers, St Padre Pio or St Charbel. We must be aware that our minds may be submerged in spiritual egotism. For example, a few weeks after Lent we are again bingeing on chocolates and forgetting to pray again. This chapter will deal with attaining the art of prayerful consistency throughout our lives.

From both my personal experience and that of young millenials and even baby boomers, there seems to be an issue with consistent commitment to prayer. Prayer is often compartmentalised into the most undervalued times of the day; for instance before sleep or even in times of trial or only even before and after Mass. When some people have tried to commit to a little more prayer and conversation with

God, they often find themselves shirking the responsibility to maintain and work on such a task. The improvements in both my personal journey of prayer, and that of numerous people around me of multiple generations, seems to support the data that I have personally collected. It thereby illustrates that one's prayer life is holistically and consistently improved by having a non-negotiable time structure to prayer times and specific itineraries for prayer activities (Divine Office, rosary, mental prayer or spiritual reading).

Let us turn our minds again to the teaching of Holy Mother Church in paragraph 1781 of the Catechism of the Catholic Church:

> *Conscience enables one to assume responsibility for the acts performed. If man commits evil, the just judgement of conscience can remain within him as the witness to the universal truth of the good, at the same time as the evil of his particular choice. The verdict of the judgement of conscience remains a pledge of hope and mercy. In attesting to the fault committed, it calls to mind the forgiveness that must be asked, the good that must still be practiced, and the virtue that must be constantly cultivated with the grace of God.*
>
> *We shall reassure our hearts before him whenever our hearts condemn us; for God is greater than our hearts, and he knows everything.*

The most radically transformative part of this paragraph is the understanding that the conscience will enable a sense of responsibility. It is in being responsible that we will learn that we must keep ourselves accountable on a consistent level, and not drift off from our everyday spiritual life in prayer. One of the hardest and most challenging aspects of our faith, especially as a young 'millennial' today, is the technology available that can dim our prayerful commitment and even distract us. Let us now equip you with the practical tools necessary to become a spiritually and prayerfully consistent person and to grow in your responsibility to persevere unto the end:

1. Create a morning, midday, evening and night routine of prayer for yourself. This will essentially act as your separable portions of holiness and sanctification of the periods of the day, as conversation with the divine must be maintained constantly. In order to genuinely implement this, you must strategise and document on paper what you aim to do specifically to the minute. It is within these essential hours that you are able to list some prayers and routines that will give a holistic shape to your life.

2. Pray the Liturgy of the Hours in the form of Lauds (Morning Prayer) after the first three weeks, then make the addition of Vespers (Evening Prayer) after the following three weeks. Finally, add Compline (Night Prayer) into your routine after an additional five weeks. You have then completed an 11-week challenge, incorporating and building structure to your prayer life.

3. Cut your personal prayer short. You heard me right. The real questions you will have for me are, why and when? Overzealousness in prayer life when we are in the 'zone' can sometimes be your egotism needing to be cut short, and sometimes it is a good form of mortification, when you feel you are on a spiritual 'high-end' that you return at a later time when emotions are better in place. Please discern and reflect on what I am saying here, before carrying this out. I also encourage you to speak with your spiritual director on this matter.

Chapter 16

How to engage in mental prayer

You have now mastered the art of consistently and effectively praying with a lower rate of spiritual complacency. Let's now approach the more challenging form of personal prayer, which you will need in order to get to know Our Lord more personally. This is what we call 'mental prayer'.

The great teacher of mental prayer, St Josemaría Escrivá, writes in *'Christ is Passing By'*, number 119:

> *Mental prayer is a heart-to-heart dialogue with God, in which the whole soul takes part; intelligence, imagination, memory and will are all involved. It is a meditation that helps to give supernatural value to our poor human life, with all its normal, everyday occurrences.*

To put it in simple terms, your mental prayer is your dialogue and conversation with Our Lord Jesus Christ in order to grow closer to Him on a personal level, resulting in a stronger personal friendship. This is called mental prayer, as Our Lord cannot speak to us in His historically physical and personal human form. He is in the form of the Eucharist, and in the people we encounter and most importantly in our souls, constituted by our intellect and will.

Therefore, it is imperative that we master our conversation with Our Lord mentally. Here are some very simple, yet challenging, practical pieces of advice that will help you get started today, and continue on this route for the rest of your life:

1. Find a suitable image of Our Lord; the ones I recommend would be a Byzantine icon or the painting by St Faustina Kowalska of the Divine Mercy image, so widely known today. There is a reason that icons in the Eastern and western Churches throughout history were used to help people pray.

2. Use this image as a source of conversation for a period of five minutes a day for the first three months and thereafter continuing to 15 minutes and after many years of mastery onto 30 minutes or more. Believe me when I say this will take some time to do well, and remember to keep false zealousness in check during your conversation.

3. Create a starting and closing prayer for your time with Our Lord, which should include checking your time on your watch or your phone. This needs to be semi-ritualised in order to create some boundaries on how and when you can converse with Our Lord on a personal level, in a conversational format. It is definitely a challenge to talk to Our Lord if you do not have enough to say, and that is why having an opening and closing prayer as boundaries will assist in doing so.

Chapter 17

Going to confession

Confession, for many people, has been a daunting and in some cases an unpleasant experience, especially if a priest has ever gotten angry at the penitent. To many, telling a man in a box all the wrong things you did can seem to be a much harder task if you have not been to confession for some time; especially when compared to directly telling Jesus your sins. Just like with anything in life, a simple fact check and brushing up on your knowledge of something can play a great part in working on the 'why' of going back more regularly, or altogether, to confession.

This sacrament is essentially applying the blood of Our Lord onto your sins and transgressions in order to wash them away as elaborated in 1 John 1:7: *'But if we walk in the light, as he is in the light, we have fellowship with one another, and the blood of Jesus his Son cleanses from all sin.'*

Our Lord commissions the apostles in John 20:22-23 with the following mission:

> *And when he said this, he breathed on them, and said to them, 'Receive the Holy Spirit. If you forgive the sins of any, they are forgiven; if you retain the sins of any, they are retained'.*

We must ask ourselves, 'What does this mean?' Because we are humans who require physical assurance and certainty, God wants to use us as humans in the priesthood (as the common faithful possess the priestly, prophetic and kingly offices through baptism) to administer His salvation.

Now let's look at getting the most out of your confession, for whichever stage you are at in your journey of faith:

1. Find a regular confessor, who should be your spiritual director. Meet the priest personally and ensure you are comfortable making a good confession.

2. Study the origins and effects of confession and revise your research one hour before and directly after. This is to ensure that the theological understanding of this sacrament is kept in mind and heart in the spirit of genuinely living the faith.

3. Assess your timeframe for confession. In consideration of others, and perhaps if it has been a while, try to book an appointment for a lengthy confession to ensure the quality of your time and spiritual advice. This is most notably to avoid occupying a large portion of the restricted time available in the public confession lines (we have all been there!). This is so that many souls can be absolved in this timeframe, especially if Mass will be taking place after and/or during confession.

Chapter 18

The art of making a good confession

Now that you have decided that you will attend confession and are driven by the spirit to approach Our Lord and seek his healing, you must now know how to effectively confess and make the most of your time with the priest. As James 5:16 says very clearly: *'Therefore confess your sins to one another, and pray for one another, that you may be healed. The prayer of a righteous man has great power in its effects'*.

It is vital to understand that confession is in a sense your eternal judgement at the hour of your death, which is fast-tracked into that confessional. Essentially you are judging yourself and showing God that you understand and are conscious of your wrongdoing in sin. You must confess that you have sinned, because Jesus Christ in the person of the priest is acting as a judge who will no longer condemn you, but will love and forgive you, under the conditions of the grace that has moved you to judge yourself as having sinned.

Please make very serious resolutions through the below practical tools to make the most out of your time in the confessional, and to leave confession each time closer to Our Lord:

1. Use the Ten Commandments as your checklist guide and look into the different forms of having broken them. Think as far back in your memory as possible (which again is why regular confession is key).

2. Write your sins down in your spiritual journal, or on a piece of paper if you would like to make this disposable after your confession; an act which is symbolic spiritually as well.

3. Attend confession every two weeks from whichever point in time you have decided to come back. I believe two weeks is a healthy balance for the average member of the laity who has not yet reached any other higher vocational levels. It can be very unhealthy to regularly attend several times a week. There needs to be some breathing space and time for penance, and over-attending can create spiritual complacency.

Chapter 19

Checking your love levels

What is love? This is a powerful word and a word that has become the most confused term in the dictionary within the context of our contemporary culture. You will hear the word 'love' all the time in the secular and Church worlds, but I believe, in order to make progress as a member of the faithful, we must understand the true meaning of love and also find ways to check if we are living a life of love. So, let us face up to this vital question today and see where love takes us and how we can make sense of it.

As paragraph 2196 of the Catechism of the Catholic Church eloquently describes:

> *In response to the question about the first of the commandments, Jesus says: 'The first is, "Hear, O Israel: The Lord our God, the Lord is one; and you shall love the Lord your God with all your heart, and with all your soul, and with all your mind, and with all your strength". The second is this, "You shall love your neighbour as*

> *yourself". There is no other commandment greater than these'.*[2]

The apostle St Paul reminds us of this in Romans 13:9-10:

> *He who loves his neighbour has fulfilled the law. The commandments, 'You shall not commit adultery, you shall not kill, you shall not steal, you shall not covet,' and any other commandment, are summed up in this sentence, 'You shall love your neighbour as yourself'. Love does no wrong to a neighbour; therefore love is the fulfillment of the law.*

Love, in simple terms, is about other people, about your neighbour and not yourself. Loving yourself is also important, in the context that you are inevitably made to transmit that to others. Love is doing what is the best for the other for the other's sake in an unconditional manner. This principle can then be extrapolated into any context of loving, for instance, with your family, friends, the community, our Lord Jesus Christ and any other avenue you can imagine.

Now, how can we check ourselves and the level of love against the standard set by Our Lord in enacting love through dying on the cross? I believe we will be assisted by the following three practical tools:

1. Ask yourself before any major decision or life project: How will this help my neighbour without seeing any returns for myself?

2. While you are sitting at Mass before the Blessed Sacrament, reflect for a minute by looking around you and thanking God for all your neighbours in the church pews.

3. When someone at work, home or in your everyday human discourse asks you for a favour, pause, and respond in your mind: 'Here I am, Lord, I come to do your will', and remember that Christ is asking through them (given the moral nature of the request).

Chapter 20

Effective catholic education

The Catholic primary and secondary education system accounts for a large portion of the worldwide schooling system. This chapter is dedicated to parents discerning the religious education for their children to grow up in the faith.

Let us start by addressing education from the parents' perspective. As the primary educators, there is a moral obligation to ensure that you pass the faith on to your children to the best of your ability, and part of managing the religious education will entail either home-schooling or sending them to school. Let us look at the teaching of the Church on this subject in paragraph 2222 of the Catechism of the Catholic Church:

> *Parents must regard their children as children of God and respect them as human persons. Showing themselves obedient to the will of the Father in heaven, they educate their children to fulfill God's law.*

Furthermore, discerning the correct method of religious education in the faith is by far the most important of all the sciences in the spirit of St Thomas Aquinas. Mathematics, science, physics, chemistry and literature can all be self-learned and are taught exceptionally well by many institutions. However, in our modern age it is difficult to find a traditional school institution that will uphold the Church's teaching, which harmoniously echoes your foundational theological and spiritual education at home.

There are three legs to the stool of Catholic formation: first and foremost, the family, then the parish or chaplaincy, and, finally, the school. The most vital way to ensure your children love Our Lord and grow to remain perpetually in the faith from a young age into adolescence is to catechise them yourselves at home. The parish can assist if it is connected to the school, but time is very limited and exposure in parish life is nothing compared to the majority of time they will be spending at school. Remember that you have one shot at getting this right, so a few kilometres, thousands of dollars per annum, and the effort will be well worth the reward you and your family will have in heaven. Remember to take very careful heed of these three practical tools and you will, God willing, raise popes and saints:

1. Ask the principal or religious education coordinator to see the religion curriculum and the demonstrated results of its relevance to catechesis and implementation. This should be indicated by the Mass attendance rate of the children after graduation, if this can be measured.

2. Take heed of which trend of school attendance prospective and current seminarians are originating from. This is very helpful to see if a school can foster vocations, which will be worth both your hard-earned money and will meet your moral obligation as parents in transmitting the faith and fostering individual vocations.

3. Speak to other practising parents, whose children have graduated from school and have successfully remained in the Church, and find out which particular schools have become the common trend. Finally, shortlist three prospective schools and decide from there.

Chapter 21

Discerning your vocation

Now on to a more personal aspect of the faith, which is to discern God's purpose for your state of life and what He has called you to fulfil in your limited time here on earth. If you think about it, the average life expectancy is something around 75 years, and I hope anyone is able to prove me wrong with a higher number. The fact of the matter is, life is short, and within this time span, Our Lord has willed and has written a life purpose in a particular state of life. However, the revelation does not come easily, but rather God creates a small puzzle, namely your vocation and what he has called you to be, and it is your job to spend the first segment of your youth or time after a conversion or reversion, in finding and piecing together the puzzle to spell out your call. Will it be marriage, the priesthood, religious or consecrated life, or blessed singleness? Only God knows, and you must find that out through both exercising faith and reason in your particular context.

Discerning this in the earliest possible stage of your life, given that you are walking the path of the Church and are tuning in to God's call, would mean that you have a moral obligation, if you know out of great conviction to make a decision about which way will ultimately help you to best attain the salvation of your soul.

I would like to take this opportunity to *clarify* that no state of life is salvifically superior to the other, and that all paths can equally provide your route to the same destination, which is heaven for all eternity. Becoming a priest or nun will not make you holier than if you have a conviction of a call to married life, as it must always be as per God's will. Let us reassure ourselves of this as stated in the Dogmatic Constitution on the Church in Lumen Gentium, paragraph 40, on the subject of the universal call to holiness:

> *The Lord Jesus, the divine Teacher and Model of all perfection, preached holiness of life to each and every one of His disciples of every condition. He Himself stands as the author and consumator of this holiness of life: 'Be you therefore perfect, even as your heavenly Father is perfect'.*

So how do you discern what state of life you are called to in this modern age of confusion? Even within the Church we can often treat discernment as a perpetual mission by never putting our foot down and making a definite decision, hence joining the 'Order of Perpetual Discerners', as they are called. Using the following practical tips, remember that we discern not to join but to take action in the state of life in the work of saving more souls:

1. Create a plan of life in prayer. To hear God's call, you must have dialogue through consistent and strong liturgical, personal and mental prayer daily. A spiritual director is necessary, so please make the effort to find one and create a path to discern this.

2. Find your talents and gifts and see which vocation they will best flourish in. This can very much assist you in weighing up, along with other factors, what God is calling you to. Some orders have a specific focus requiring particular talents that you can consider in your decision making.

3. Research through practical and first-hand experience. If you do not know what a priest, friar, married person or single person does, then please spend time understanding what they do. This will provide you with greater clarity to see if you will be fit to undertake this calling for the rest of your life.

Chapter 22

How to discern marriage

Marriage is by far the vocation to which most of the faithful are called to. We all have the desire for love and finding our fulfilment in God alone, through the means and example of another charming individual. Marriage and family are the measure of a healthy Church, so radically that all the other vocations depend on it as a stabilising foundation. There is no escape from the reality that the reason for the shortage of vocations and the shocking statistics of the practice of the faith among youth is due to the faith not being passed on by the leadership within the family — namely, the parents.

Marriage always starts between both a husband and a wife who both love God and each other. We have all heard the saying, 'It takes three to get married'. This is why the Catechism of the Catholic Church in paragraph 1616 states the following point about this sacrament:

> *This is what the Apostle Paul makes clear when he says: 'Husbands, love your wives, as Christ loved the Church*

and gave himself up for her, that he might sanctify her,' adding at once: *'For this reason a man shall leave his father and mother and be joined to his wife, and the two shall become one. This is a great mystery in reference to Christ and the Church'.*

Most men and women - assuming they are well-formed and practising Catholics - seem to be influenced by elements of living in chastity and even materialism. From my observations over the past decade, I can confidently say that many men and women of faith face obstacles, and here are your practical solutions to overcoming them if you want to walk down the aisle with confidence:

1. Formulate a regular routine of prayer together on both your dates and time together. This is vital for staying together and overcoming any obstacle in your way. I recommend the rosary for chastity, the Mass as often as possible, and most importantly adoration of the Blessed Sacrament. One of these practices should always be incorporated on every single date night or prolonged time together.

2. Talk about finance. Many practising, newly-wedded couples have often realised after they walk down the aisle that they discover bad financial habits about their significant other or about themselves. There are poor saving habits, investment prospects, an underestimation of living costs and overspending habits. Though such faith-filled marriages may not break down, it will make the ride bumpier and harder for your way of life, and will inevitably affect your living conditions or how many children you are able to glorify God with. Furthermore, consider what Catholic education costs and options you will have for your children. Please have an open and honest discussion, even disclosing savings and statements prior to discerning engagement. It is also prudent to

propose at the right time when all finances are at a good level.

3. Ensure that both parties are not bringing in any unhealthy habits or addictions into your marriage. For any issues, see an appropriate professional and rectify the situation before any sort of engagement. You can be sure that these things cannot be swept under the rug, as they will also walk down the aisle with you on your special day and affect your marriage.

Chapter 23

How to date catholic style

Dating has become one of the most confused concepts within western civilisation in the past few decades; there is confusion about the entire etiquette and process. Historically, dating etiquette was scarcely practised by previous generations and has not been passed on as a result. Unfortunately, the Church and its people have not been spared from this social upheaval, and we too as a faith community need to understand how to implement some practical guidelines when it comes to dating or courting.

Let me first start with a disclaimer that what I am about to instruct you in are some guidelines that would have to be discerned and adapted to your particular situation. There is no 'one size fits all' for everybody, as people find themselves in many different situations. In order to successfully date as a Catholic, you must have the end goal in mind, which is why we must turn our attention to the ultimate goal as explained by St Paul in Ephesians 5:22-25:

> *Wives, be subject to your husbands, as to the Lord. For the husband is the head of the wife as Christ is the head of the Church, his body, and is himself its saviour. As the Church is subject to Christ, so let wives also be subject in everything to their husbands. Husbands, love your wives, as Christ loved the Church and gave himself up for her.*

This is, therefore, the standard of love that we are aiming to achieve, not to simply get a dose of self-esteem when we attain a highly-coveted phone number or when we are able to impress that fair lady.

Let's define the two most important terms vital to our progress in this area:

Dating: Is an exclusive or regular form of keeping company between members of the opposite sex, in order to discern a possible long-term relationship for a period of time prior to marriage. This is often colloquially used to describe people already in long-term relationships. Dating for several weeks or months is a good timeframe, depending on the exposure to one another, before finally making a decision whether both parties find it prudent to enter into a courting relationship to discern marriage. Such dating must not be carried out casually, but with the end goal in mind, which is marriage. For without a goal, there is confusion.

Courting: Is once several dates have taken place and both parties find that they are compatible. Making the relationship official would then technically be referred to as 'courting' until marriage.

In order to succeed in dating, please apply the following and I can guarantee you will not fall short of a successful dating dynamic:

1. Set a foundation of at least one month of friendship.

In whatever situation you find yourselves, if you have met somebody in a group setting and will regularly be exposed to each other, it is imperative to spend the equivalent of one to two months — depending on how much exposure there is — before entering the dating stage discussed above. This will save you time, energy, and emotional distress and will assist you in discerning someone objectively, with no attachments or emotions, before you go into uncharted waters.

2. Ensure you are prepared to begin the dating stage discussed above. For example, if you are in high school, starting university or any other life situation, and marriage is not foreseeable within the next three to four years from this point in time, then you should not engage in a relationship. Hence you should remain friends within the context of a wider social setting and not date exclusively.

3. Ensure that every single date has an element of prayer within it. I highly recommend that you make a visit to the Blessed Sacrament or find a perpetual adoration chapel; this will also tell you something about the prayer life of that particular person. There is nothing better than bringing them before Our Lord.

Chapter 24

Dating etiquette (dating secrets revealed)

Surely, I was not going to send you out on your first date without more specific and practical guidelines! Please enjoy and take very seriously the following practical guidelines. If you execute the below correctly, you will be giving glory to God, as God does not accept faulty sacrifice, as stated in Leviticus 22:20: *'You shall not offer anything that has a blemish, for it will not be acceptable for you'*.

We must see all our daily activities done well as giving glory to and offering sacrifice to Our Lord. Furthermore, on a personal note, the following etiquette will display a great sense of character.

Should proceeding to the dating stage be appropriate, what I call the 'Dating Dynamics' should consist of the following checklist, which should be easily applicable in western civilisation (at least once you have read this chapter):

- The man will find a suitable place which is within

budget and which is quiet, to ensure that a thorough conversation can be undertaken, as this would be a first date.

- The man, by phone or in person, asks the woman on a date with a minimum notice period of one week, and arrangements are then made to pick her up (assuming with a vehicle). Details of the dress code will be provided by the man.
- Both parties should be dressed appropriately and modestly.
- The man should arrive at the woman's house a minimum of 15 minutes prior to the scheduled time, and conversely the woman should be ready at this time also. The man must knock on the door, and if the woman still resides with either or both of her parents, he should respectfully introduce himself and ask if they would kindly allow him to take their daughter for a date, with an intended return time of no later than 10:30pm (it may vary depending on the customs of your cultural background).
- The etiquette techniques observed: The man opens both the car door and building door for the woman, then he proceeds to pull the chair out for the woman, providing her with the seat with the best view. Furthermore, when the pair are walking on the footpath, the man should walk on the side of the road at all times.
- Chastity guidelines: The dating stage does in no way, shape or form entitle you to any form of affection, as this is an initial probationary discernment for both parties.
- Questions and conversation: This is a time to ask about all the simple and basic details of the person, and to dive deeper into their life of faith, interests and personality. Objection signs and red flags should always be noted by both parties.
- After several dates: We all know what the 'third date' means. It means for us as faithful Catholics it is time

to make a decision, if we have known the person for at least one month as friends and then have spent three dates to discover deeper truths about the other. It is time to finally make a decision and be open on a face-to-face level and to define the relationship if both parties would like to proceed to courtship or close the dating stage with the conclusion that it is best to leave it at that.

- Despite which decision is observed, all the necessary etiquette discussed above is applicable. Remember, for any situation and whichever way it goes, there is always something to be gained and you can only grow and benefit from this situation, despite what your emotions might say.

Chapter 25

Filtering out western sexualisation

We live in a heavily sexualised culture that does not seek to spare anyone. This is evident from the readily available pornography, hook-up culture, school and media indoctrination, and all the other tactics employed by the progressive and liberalised culture. You too will not be spared, and perhaps have not been spared, if you do not engage with this chapter and spend time reflecting upon tackling this in your personal life.

There is nothing more fitting than the instruction of scripture from 1 Peter 5:8-10:

> *Be sober, be watchful. Your adversary the devil prowls around like a roaring lion, seeking someone to devour. Resist him, firm in your faith, knowing that the same experience of suffering is required of your brotherhood throughout the world. And after you have suffered a little while, the God of all grace, who has called you to his eternal glory in Christ, will himself restore, establish, and strengthen you.*

In order to tackle the sexualisation of the West, we need to fight the obvious signs and temptations before us. However, the most damaging effects are the slow and unnoticed or subliminal influence that it will have on your life. For example, the media, music, pop culture, radio stations, commercials and most notably the modern movies of today. Now, I am not a party pooper, but we need to find some practical measures to still enjoy what is good in our modern society without allowing the smoke of Satan to infect our temple. As such, I have come up with three very simple strategies, which, if implemented well, will create your shield against sexual temptation:

1. Cut out your exposure to commercials and mainstream 'fake news' media. By doing this you will reduce the amount of nonsense that affects your subconscious. I recommend subscribing to digital television so that you can choose what you watch, instead of being exposed to commercials and other reports designed to deceive or even tempt.

2. Download and subscribe to music outlets where you can choose music and create a playlist. Please discern the music and its emotional implications on your actions, along with the lyrics. This will help you keep thoughts or temptations at bay.

3. Stay away or discern attending events and places where a lack of physical modesty is prevalent. Music festivals and other beach-related events almost always tempt both men and women, and it is important to keep both memories and participation distant from them.

Chapter 26

Discerning a Vocation to the Priesthood

Currently, we have a shortage of priests within our western nations. However, there are a steady number of priests and vocations growing in the Middle East, Africa and Asia, which can be attributed to the faith of those regions. What I would like to bring to your attention is the deficiencies in the systematic approach to discerning vocations that I have personally experienced and witnessed over the past 12 years.

We have established that all the faithful of the Church are called to seek and work for the salvation of their souls, and the universal call to holiness. It is a bottom-line call for every person to practise the faith, attend Mass, pray and do penance. These are bottom-line Catholic principles, and are in no way exclusively for a priest to live, as we are all on the same spiritual boat and will all be judged before the throne of God at the end of our lives.

So, what makes a priest different in his calling and function?

The primary role of a priest from all religions throughout all different civilisations, even within our own time, is to offer sacrifice to a deity on behalf of the people whom he represents. If you have watched a film about the Aztecs, ancient Celtic people or the Roman Empire, you would have seen numerous offerings and sacrifices being offered to the gods for rain, hail or shine. There is just something embedded within human nature that brings us to offer sacrifices and gifts.

In Exodus 28:3-4 we find the identity of the priesthood coming to fruition, in order to offer sacrifice and hence worship the one true God:

> *And you shall speak to all who have ability, whom I have endowed with an able mind, that they make Aaron's garments to consecrate him for my priesthood.*

Furthermore, it is on this very foundation of the Levitical priesthood that Our Lord institutes the 12 apostles, representing the 12 tribes of Israel (Matthew 19:28). The reason I mention this is because you almost never hear about this in your mainstream discernment programs, and if you are to succeed in any vocation or life project, a basic principle of life is that you understand the identity of anything you are undertaking.

The reason I stress the effective discernment process is to keep an open mind and to always think for yourself. This is because we often see a rotating door in seminaries, due to the lack of a concrete discernment process. This may even occur in the seminary, where Our Lord will let you know that it may not be His will at that point in time. Discerning more effectively and making the best decision possible, will help you to answer God's call and aid you in minimising any time lost for yourself and the seminary. The key to remember is that the seminary is only a means to the real job after ordination; that the seven years will run by quickly and your real call is to the priesthood and not the seminary.

To discern if a man is to enter the seminary or a religious order and discern the priesthood, he must immerse himself in the identity of the priest, and not vaguely settle for the idea of 'serving God' or 'helping people', which every human being, let alone a Catholic, is called to do anyway. It is simply not enough to rest on these ideas, and this is why I have devised a threefold criteria for every man discerning the priesthood:

1. Meditate and ask yourself through your discernment process, always cross-checking every step or idea with these questions: Am I called to offer sacrifice to God on behalf of the people through offering the sacrifice of the Mass and absolving the faithful through confession? Is this unique call to carry this activity out the sole purpose of my vocation and not just deriving from the love of the Mass (which every Catholic must have anyway)?

2. Find a spiritual director, permanent or temporary for the discernment period, who is a good and faithful priest and has demonstrated a profound understanding of his purpose and vocation, with at least 10 to 15 years' experience. Let him be your guide until your ultimate decision is reached.

3. Put a timeframe on discerning first, and if you are certain, apply for the seminary. If you continue with life and leave this question open, then put another timeframe on this, and come to a decision that should direct the course of the rest of your life. If you are in doubt, and the voice from Our Lord for the seminary is not certain, there is no harm; perhaps it may be God's will for you at this time that you continue with secular work and gain further experience in the real world.

If you later enter the seminary and reach ordination, the skills you have gained will aid you in the work of managing a parish and effectively delivering results for the people of God. No skills are ever lost.

Chapter 27

Discerning a Consecrated or Religious Vocation

Now let's talk about the way to know if you are called to religious life. Although I have no personal experience discerning religious life, I have developed an understanding personally through the years in conversations and through my radio program. I will hopefully assist you with this in the best means possible.

Let's now turn to Ephesians 4:10-12, where we can reflect on the different roles and functions that Our Lord has created within His body:

> *He who descended is he who also ascended far above all the heavens, that he might fill all things. And his gifts were that some should be apostles, some prophets, some evangelists, some pastors and teachers, to equip the saints for the work of ministry, for building up the body of Christ.*

What is vital to understand is the fact that the religious are called to live three things: poverty, chastity and obedience; hence my three practical tools for this subject in discerning will be very direct and applicable, as follows:

1. Find your spirituality. List all the orders that you may be attracted to, and then finally narrow it down to your top three. Then spend time discerning with each order individually with no commitment or entrance as yet. This will give you a distance-view of the order. Please ensure, in light of the social and spiritual upheaval of the Church, to find an order that is doctrinally and spiritually orthodox. If you are to profess obedience to a superior and live within an order that has questionable beliefs or practices, you will be damaging your soul, and I do not say this lightly.

2. Check your general compatibility with most of the members of the order, as having a different mindset or personality that clashes with others in the community will be like marrying someone whom you cannot get along with, and that would not make much sense either. In reality, if you are joining a community, you must be able to personally adapt to the community, especially if you are bound by obedience.

3. Start practising your poverty by reducing your material items. Do a usual stocktake of items you no longer need, and sell them to pawn shops or by any other means, and donate the money to the poor. This is a principle in which I have seen a consistent response from many religious. This practice will assist in your detachment from the world. I would also recommend refraining from investing or any other emotionally-dense financial decisions during your discernment process.

Chapter 28

Discerning a Life of Blessed Singleness

Now to a more personal issue which many find very awkward to address - a life of blessed singleness. It doesn't exist. What I mean is that being single and doing nothing for God nor serving his people doesn't exist. Every human being is called to give his life for Christ and for others, even if they are not called to the married, priestly or religious states. It is important to note that being single is not a ticket out of serving God. Not everyone is called to be married, priestly or religious, however, some are called to be single and growing in holiness in their everyday life, giving glory to God through their work.

People who are in the state of singleness have a much more demanding mission; that is, to achieve more results for the glory of God and his Church. If you are someone who works in a secular profession and you have no one to answer to on an everyday level, that would mean you have much greater levels of freedom to achieve impeccable things that others in their various states of life could not possibly achieve. Some of the greatest politicians, teachers, doctors, lawyers and many more professionals have all been single. It is just simply an opportunity to capitalise on the time given to you to serve the Church, especially in this difficult time. Singleness is your gift from God to get more done for his kingdom while you are here on earth.

There is a great parallel between the priesthood and religious life, and that of someone who discerns to live a life of blessed singleness. The very time, energy and love that the priests, religious or even consecrated virgins are able to devote to the people of God, has elements of a single individual in the secular world. Being single allows you to direct much more energy into serving Christ through your ordinary circumstances in your profession. Further, this also allows you to be completely free to aid the pastoral needs of the Church through both your parish life or any organisation of which you may discern God is asking you to be a part of. Given the average life expectancy, there is very little time to do penance, and to work to make the Church and the world a better place, and to positively impact the lives of others.

I have been guided by several exceptional people in my life. The common denominator in the guidance and formation that they have eloquently transmitted unto me, and that I am aspiring to implement, has been that they do not have the commitment of a family and children. This has been applicable to those who may not have been blessed with children and are married. There is much work to be done in our time of restoring the Church through catechising the faithful, to see greater numbers of people attending Mass again.

Listen to what St Paul says to all the singles out there in 1 Corinthians 7:8: *'To the unmarried and the widows I say that it is well for them to remain single as I do'*. If you reflect upon the amount of work that St Paul did for the people of God and the subsequent results that he achieved within his lifetime, one would only naturally imagine what St Paul was capable of. Had he decided to marry and have a family, what would that have looked like? Would we have seen as many massive conversions to the faith? Would all his letters have ever been written, when his wife was pregnant and he was morally obliged to support her? Or would he have retired from his ministry altogether? It is hard to say, but what we know is that it would have definitely limited his outreach. This is why I am passionate about people who are not called to marriage to have a changed attitude towards your life, and to take action now with the three following practical tools to optimise your time and serve Our Lord and his Church:

1. Consider running for government or getting involved in a political party. I only say 'consider' in the case that you may or may not be suitable for this. However, if you are a well-rounded individual who is practising your faith, and who has determined your years in singleness, your time will be well-utilised. In the modern world of confusion today, your voice in parliament or in a political party will help to bring conscience to the floor within your domain. The reason I say this is because Catholic political involvement can be very difficult today, requiring time and great emotional energy, which is why people who are single, who are willing and capable, might find this to be an option.

2. Start a weekly to monthly faith formation program, or support one that may already exist in your parish. Take hold of speakers and media resources, and perhaps even present them in order to respond to the catechetical crisis in the Church. Imagine the great spiritual and personal satisfaction that you will receive once you see tens to hundreds of your parishioners and faithful come back and grow in their faith because of the fruits of your labour. Just let that thought resonate with you, and while it's only an added benefit, your primary result will be giving glory to God.

3. Mentor young adults professionally and spiritually. This can be a very helpful tool for you to invest your time over coffee or a beer in assisting as many people as possible, which will bring great joy and assistance to needy souls. This could possibly be in the form of a youth or young adult group, which would ultimately provide great assistance for those needing direction in life.

Chapter 29

How to select a spiritual director

I remember the experience many years ago of leaving a dinner table, apologising to a group of people who were born-again Christians and explaining that I would be seeing my 'spiritual director'. You can only imagine the facial expressions before I clarified that I was not going to a high-rise building with a man in a black suit and cigar in his hand. The term 'director' sounds very impressive, and rightly so, when you see consistent and organic growth in your spiritual life over time. Paragraph 2690 of the Catechism of the Catholic Church defines and explains what a spiritual director is:

> *The Holy Spirit gives to certain of the faithful the gifts of wisdom, faith and discernment for the sake of this common good which is prayer (spiritual direction). Men and women so endowed are true servants of the living tradition of prayer ... If the spiritual director has no experience of the spiritual life, he will be incapable of leading into it the souls whom God is calling to it, and he will not even understand them.*

Over the past decade, my experiences in many different aspects of Church life have enabled me to devise a threefold practical approach to selecting a spiritual director for exclusive mentorship. In most cases, this should be a priest or a member of the laity, depending on the Church organisation to which they belong.

1. Find an accessible and available person no further than a 40-minute commute from your work or home. When someone is too far from home or has a very tight schedule, or both for that matter, we can be easily discouraged from seeing them and will frequently delay spiritual direction at the pleasure of the enemy. That would be identical to a military officer being inaccessible to the men under his command, which, in the context of a spiritual battle, will not have a pleasant outcome.

2. Ensure they have a minimum of 10 years' experience (with a tolerance of one year if they have been reputable) as a spiritual director, and perhaps find out from others who they have mentored how helpful they have been in their spiritual progress.

3. Ensure they are someone with whom you have no personal friendship, as this is a serious spiritual conflict of interest. However, it would be advantageous if they have known you for several years.

Chapter 30

How to get involved and change your parish

You may find yourself in your lifelong parish or one you have joined recently. This may not be an overly vibrant community with a flourishing laity in the faith and you wish to assist your parish priest and community in reviving and improving what I call the 'three dimensions of parish life': the catechetical, liturgical and pastoral.

Let us reflect on assisting the body of Christ in the context of the faithful in the following passage from paragraph 798 of the Catechism of the Catholic Church:

> *By baptism, through which he forms Christ's Body; by the sacraments, which give growth and healing to Christ's members; by 'the grace of the apostles, which holds first place among his gifts'; by the virtues, which make us act according to what is good; finally, by the many special graces (called 'charisms'), by which he makes the faithful 'fit and ready' to undertake various tasks and offices for the renewal and building up of the Church.*

What we need to understand are our personal charisms and talents in order to aid the parish life, and what you can bring to the table of the Lord. I have often heard many people complain about how a liturgical, catechetical, or any pastoral affair is handled in the parish, and then not proceed to be part of creating a solution. This is often a result of their lack of enthusiasm, or their disenchantment. However, there is no longer any more time left in our present crisis to stay silent and inactive. For the next five to ten years, society will change rapidly, and there is no longer a moment to spare in repairing the crisis on a parish level. Therefore, I leave you with some very serious instructions about how you can take action and bring your skills to the table for your parish or parishes:

1. Seek to join or assist your Parish Pastoral Council. All major decisions are usually suggested to the parish priest in this important body. If you want to be highly effective in making changes and enhancing the progress of your parish, do not delay any further and take action in this area by speaking to your parish priest.

2. Create youth, young adults and adult faith formation groups in your parish. Advertise these in your parish bulletin and ensure you are able to have leaders for each division. There are numerous Catholic talks and lectures by credible clergy and academics worldwide, which you could even showcase as an alternative to having live speakers.

3. Seek an external Catholic point of view from a trusted apostolate. Having an external analysis of the condition and evangelical performance of your parish from someone who has no emotional investment is part of the key to finding an objective solution. Just like all major organisations always like to see the correct perspective through a different lens, the parish need not be run any differently.

Parish formation essentials:

The three pillars of formation for a Catholic from the moment of birth unto the final days of one's life, that will shape the soul of the individual, are the family, school and finally, the parish. Our focus will be on nurturing a parish life, to achieve its ultimate objective. The parish is a physical community with its own territorial boundary within the diocese to which it belongs, in most cases. This is your local community of the faithful where you can find access to the sacraments, a priest, and be in communion with Our Lord and the other members of his body.

In the modern world, parishes are struggling to engage the faithful who belong to its community. They consist of many people who were cradle Catholics and who are continuing the 'tradition' of attending Sunday Mass, because it was just something that was always done and it is also good for the kids. We find this can be a prominent attitude among Mass-goers, that we can even refer to them as '59 Catholics' — Catholics who attend Mass and leave, and have no living faith beyond the communion line. This challenge particularly daunts many priests and staff of that community, often leaving them clueless as to how they can re-engage the people who still remain in the pews every week; and in light of an ageing population, what future would be imminent given the often poor engagement of youth and fostering of vocations that we witness today. Here are three practical projects that every parish priest or parishioner can work towards together:

1. Sacralise your liturgy again. This is by far the aspect of parish life that most often gets swept under the rug of our neglect and ignorance. The sole purpose of our worship and the very reason for which we gather on Sunday needs to be in check. If we treat our liturgy with reverence, from sacred furnishings, music, gestures and other elements, the parishioners will be elevated greatly to God. Think about it this way: why would

someone respect the Church, and the faith altogether, if we do not even take our Mass seriously? Eliminating unnecessary entertainment from the Mass, and putting God at the centre of worship, will provide a greater identity for people to continue practising the faith.

2. Create a youth and young adult group. The youth are simply the future of the Church, and due to the complimentary collaboration with the schooling system to which they belong, they have a greater chance of receiving catechesis and formation. Especially with young adults who are asking crucial questions during our modern time, if we are not competing for the souls and minds of the youth, the secular world will inevitably win.

3. Create a parish catechetical formation program. To compliment the upgrade of your liturgy, you must then explain the changes, and also the faith, through creating a monthly to bimonthly formation program. If you are to make any liturgical changes to your everyday Masses, it is vital to keep your parishioners informed. This basic information must act as a catechesis and education for why, for example, some furnishings are being changed. Information sessions and also written notices of changes should be both distributed and also made available online. Every successful parish must absolutely have this in its cycle of activities.

Chapter 31

The art of catholic business networking

The reason I have chosen this topic is simply because of the reality that we rarely hear this spoken of in the Church's society today. There are professional breakfasts, however, we rarely hear about Catholics networking with each other for business purposes. After all, we are capitalists who work for the glory of God and can help other like-minded faithful with any professional or entrepreneurial endeavours.

Here is an example in Acts 7:9-10, which recounts the story of Joseph and his ascent to power because of his networking skills and wisdom:

> *And the patriarchs, jealous of Joseph, sold him into Egypt; but God was with him, and rescued him out of all his afflictions, and gave him favour and wisdom before Pharaoh, king of Egypt, who made him governor over Egypt and over all his household.*

Joseph was able to win a victory for the people of Israel

and enable them to flourish in Egyptian society. Perhaps we can assume that this alliance with the pharaoh would have flourished further had they shared the same mission in life driven by one common faith. It is precisely from recalling the life of Joseph and his personal success that I envision faithful Catholics uniting together in business, professional and political matters to personally flourish and assist the propagation of the faith. When Christendom is united, it is an unstoppable force; but when it is divided, the result is manifested in tragic events such as the fall of Constantinople.

For Christendom to flourish, Catholic business owners, professionals, politicians and developers can inspire others of the faithful and assist them with the same aspirations through the three following practical measures:

1. Practising Catholics should procure services in all aspects of their lives to the best of their abilities from other practising Catholics. In short, support our fellow faithful. If you don't have any pre-existing or important clientele relationships for services offered by accountants, doctors, lawyers or any other professional, seek fellow faithful Catholics in every procurement move. This is not a moral obligation by any means, but if you are going to hand over your money to someone, I beg of you, consider giving it to a fellow member of the faithful, given they will provide a quality service as the main priority.

2. If you do not know anyone, find someone who is a practising Catholic and allow them to act as a directory for you, should you require any services in the future. This is a foundational principle in networking that you should heed. For example, there was a time when I needed to procure an electrician, plumber and carpenter for our outdoor kitchen. I did not know of any practising faithful among those professions at the time, so a fellow parishioner recommended

some. As a result, I sourced moral and competitive individuals who completed exceptional work; and I had supported hard-working, faithful families. I could have easily carried out a Google search, but in this situation, there was a two-fold benefit.

3. Ask your parish priest to create a business directory of people who are known to be committed faithful, with an interview-like process before being added to the directory to ensure they are practising Catholics and are not simply disguised as parishioners. In turn, should the parish require any of these services, a message for clergy reading this is to have these businesses as your first point of contact and preference. At the end of the day, your personal interests of price, quality and honesty are what take precedence. If all these factors are found in your fellow faithful, then I rest my case.

Chapter 32

Guidelines for Catholic youth groups

My return back to the Catholic faith was aided by studying the doctrine of the Church, and this took place in my early high school years. As a young person, I had witnessed the youth groups and young adult discussion nights, which were not appealing to me at the time. I never had an appreciation of them, nor did I see the great need for anything to foster young people's faith, other than the study of 'The Summa' and Cardinal Joseph Ratzinger's works. Coming back to the faith through study is what has shaped my youth group experience, and has allowed me to advise the foundation of youth groups that have successfully achieved what I call the 'Catholic youth equilibrium'. This is a balance of both engaging and entertaining young people with relevance to our culture, to then foster inclusiveness in a group. This proceeds to nurture the community with clear catechesis for the youth, who are then exposed to Church dogma and moral teaching relevant to their social situation and struggles, with real-world practical skills, if the youth group is capable. This needs to be the only objective of every youth group in order to achieve the Church's desired outcome of fostering and catechising the youth.

What anyone can observe is that there are times in which youth and young adult groups are either exclusively or overly-focused on either study of the faith or on engaging and entertaining the group, to the exclusion of the other. Both are necessary, in order to create purpose through knowing the faith and community-building side-by-side.

Let us now be encouraged by the words of St Pope John Paul II in *Dilecti Amici*, Paragraph 1, which exalts youth to recognise the importance of this stage of life. This could be a guide for youth group leaders guiding our future generations, as he states:

> *Since man is the fundamental and at the same time the daily way of the Church, it is easy to understand why the Church attributes special importance to the period of youth as a key stage in the life of every human being. You young people are the ones who embody this youth: you are the youth of the nations and societies, the youth of every family and of all humanity; you are also the youth of the Church. We are all looking to you, for all of us, thanks to you, in a certain sense continually becoming young again. So your youth is not just your own property, your personal property or the property of a generation: it belongs to the whole of that space that every man traverses in his life's journey, and at the same time it is a special possession belonging to everyone. It is a possession of humanity itself.*

Therefore, young people who would either act as youth leaders or attendees must heed the words of our Roman Pontiff, when he stressed that your youth is not your own property. Being young does not give you an excuse to shirk responsibility or live for your own self every day of those years. Your energy, initiatives and time should be given as a gift to God, and to others around you. Furthermore, I would even argue that your youth is an obligation to serve in greater capacity, since, when you are young and have the energy, time and zeal for your passions, you must align them to the will of God and the work he intends you to carry out, with your unique gifts and talents. In the context of running a youth group specifically, here are some very practical tools for each leader, to implement in their checklist:

1. Ensure that you have a strong catechetical program, which would be broken up according to relevant age groups, using online Catholic-approved resources and even live speakers. Once you create a strong culture, engage numerous youth to start with as the foundation of a group within your parish.

2. Ensure you bring older and wiser speakers to give a talk at your youth group. The aims of a youth or young adult group should include young people growing up and maturing, and not simply over-celebrating adolescence. It would then be ideal to incorporate the wisdom of wiser and older people. This is a very serious problem I have found over the years; that in many cases we have not inspired the young to grow up faster, but only to enjoy being young for the sake of it, which needs to be better understood and addressed.

3. Individual mentorship. It is hard for youth leaders to have a chance to focus on the needs, questions or emotions of one particular member. That is why discussion groups could take place during a session and the leaders could have a one-on-one chat with each member to see how they are progressing. This complements the sense of community growth, by fostering each individual as a building block of that very community.

Chapter 33

Catholic cultural etiquette not to forget

Catholic cultural etiquette is something I have personally been very interested in, and I pay great attention to the minor details within the liturgy. I believe all Catholics reading this should adhere to some of the most basic etiquette rules that are applicable in the Latin Rite (common to most of the faithful), which will help to foster your sense of reverence and uniformity within the faith. We will learn in this context some ground rules for the Church and its hierarchy, which I believe have been lost heavily over the past four decades, and that we should be working to restore.

Church etiquette:

1. Genuflection: Is bending your right knee, which belongs to the Blessed Sacrament when it is not exposed, during Mass, before taking your seat or passing by the tabernacle, which is usually behind the centre of the altar.

2. Double genuflection: Is simply bowing while kneeling on the floor. This is done when the Blessed Sacrament is exposed.

3. Bowing: When the name of Jesus is said within a liturgical context, bow to a consecrated altar. When the celebrant processes in and out of the holy sacrifice of the Mass we bow to them, as the priest is acting *'in persona Christi'*, or in the person of Christ.

Catholic cultural etiquette:

1. Greeting the Pope or a Bishop: Genuflect using your left knee (as the right knee is reserved for Our Lord only) to the Bishop once grabbing hold of his hand; it would be optional to kiss his hand at the same time, as is customary in some countries.

2. Hierarchical titles:
   Deacon – Deacon
   Priest – Father
   Monsignor – Monsignor
   Bishop – Your Lordship
   Archbishop (metropolitan Archdiocese) – Your Grace
   Papal Nuncio – Your Excellency
   Cardinal – Your Eminence
   Pope – Your Holiness
   Nun – Sister
   Women's Religious Superior – Mother
   Religious Brother – Brother

Chapter 34

Supporting catholic homosexuals

This is probably one of the most underwritten pastoral topics in the Church today; without achieving what I like to call the 'Catholic and pastoral equilibrium'. We can often get too conservative about what the Church teaches on this subject and not open ourselves to truly loving individuals and to sharing the mercy and healing of Christ. However, when we approach the situation in this light, we can also be enticed to throw the baby out with the bath water and sideline the law of God, thereby not calling the individuals to live a life of chastity, which they are called to live.

That is why this section will deal with very practical elements of exercising the 'mercy' and 'compassion' that we so often talk about, without compromising what Holy Mother Church infallibly teaches about this subject.

The way to start tackling this issue is to enhance our attitude and perspective regarding homosexuality. We must understand that all individuals of different sexualities are called to live chastely, and in no way in dealing with the issue of homosexuality at this time and place are we singularly targeting this issue. We often talk about other struggles in chastity, such as pornography, infidelity, masturbation or any other struggle or situation. We simply love all people who are sinners and we are striving to assist them with whatever struggles they have, helping them to grow. However, for individuals who find themselves with homosexual tendencies, I would like to remind you of your special calling to carry your cross and live a life of chastity and good example for others.

Despite the loud and aggressive voices of the media labelling the Church as homophobic and discriminatory, let us put such nonsense to bed and state directly from the words of that same Holy Mother Church what we actually teach regarding this subject from the Catechism of the Catholic Church in paragraph 2357:

> *Homosexuality refers to relations between men or between women who experience an exclusive or predominant sexual attraction toward persons of the same sex. It has taken a great variety of forms through the centuries and in different cultures. Its psychological genesis remains largely unexplained. Basing itself on Sacred Scripture, which presents homosexual acts as acts of grave depravity, tradition has always declared that 'homosexual acts are intrinsically disordered'. They are contrary to the natural law. They close the sexual act to the gift of life. They do not proceed from a genuine affective and sexual complementarity. Under no circumstances can they be approved.*

The Church has clearly stated that these acts are gravely disordered because of a simple fact — that they are against the natural law. They are breaking an order within nature, in keeping with the language of Catholic philosophy. Let us finally immerse ourselves in three practical ways we as

Catholics are able to support our fellow homosexual faithful, friends or community members:

1. Set up a meeting time. If a person with same-sex attraction is willing to discuss the Church's teaching, explain the above paragraph of the Catechism and take them through a journey of understanding the Church's actual teaching. Then proceed to juxtapose this with the mainstream media lies and deception, which misrepresents the Church as discriminatory and homophobic. Most of the time when things are clarified, true progress and healing can be achieved.

2. Make sure to create these meetings individually, then speak to your parish priest to possibly create a larger scale support group, supervised by orthodox and catechised laity and clergy. Relevant approval will be required, which is why a constitution or objective layout must be set up, to ensure groups like this do not get out of hand.

3. Supply your fellow homosexual faithful, family, friends or community members with Church resources by reputable speakers for them to undergo personal research on this subject. This will provide what I like to call the 'homework effect', allowing autonomous research and reflection about why the Church loves everyone and calls us all (not just homosexual individuals) to salvation.

Chapter 35

Dressing modestly for women

As a man, I cannot personally address the topic on how women should dress modestly. I have asked the co-founder and creative director of The Catholic Toolbox *and* The Rite of Manhood, *Akita Sanchez, to address this matter. Akita was trained in fashion design and worked as a designer for several years. She also provides three practical tips on how to live out modesty in your everyday life:*

Many people think modesty is defined as being shy, timid or limited in what is being given. What we need to understand is that modesty exists as a way of showcasing our inner beauty without giving away our dignity. It is not only demonstrated by how we dress, but includes certain attributes such as our attitudes, the way we speak, whether we think critically, our sense of style and how we do certain things.

Modesty is one of the fruits of the Holy Spirit, as stated in St Paul's letter to the Galatians (5:16-26). What we know about the fruits of the Holy Spirit is that there is usually a counterpart that can be seen as 'not obtaining the kingdom of God'. Modesty's counterpart is, unsurprisingly, immodesty.

Within the last century, fashion has changed and evolved drastically. It was only since the 1920s that women's fashion started to become more 'rebellious', swimming into androgynous style. Coco Chanel was one of the first designers to create fashion that was considered different, but which is now quite common in the modern era. For example, Coco admired her boyfriend's clothes and began to wear his clothing. She began to fashion clothing for women inspired by manly attributes, which would eventually create a ripple effect in getting women to wear pants.

Pants were classified as a questionable item in a woman's wardrobe back in the day. To stay modest, women typically wore dresses or skirts that did not highlight certain body parts, such as their limbs. In the modern-day era, we see women and even young teenagers dressed with such little fabric because it is deemed as 'cute'. What is not 'cute' is the fact that this attracts the wrong kind of attention, especially from the opposite gender. There is a fine line between modesty and immodesty.

St John Paul II states that there is a time and a place to wear certain items of clothing. For example, you would wear a swimsuit to the beach, but you would not wear it to a formal dinner. What we need to remember in these modern times is that when you dress, you choose to communicate to the world certain attributes about yourself without saying a single word.

One of my personal pet peeves is when people choose not to dress appropriately for Mass. The term 'Sunday best' was coined because people used to make their best effort to dress for attending Mass on Sunday. Now you do not need to wear an expensive outfit to wear your 'Sunday best' to

Mass, but consider how you would dress if you are about to meet royalty. If you had the Queen over for tea, what would you wear? When we go to Mass we need to be mindful that we are meeting *Christus Rex*, or Christ the King. You would at least wear something sensible, clean and perhaps ironed! The King does not want to see your bosom, an outline of your legs or your muscly arms! The King demands respect from you!

In my lifetime, I have admired certain trends that come and go. As a woman, I love updating my wardrobe with seasonal pieces. However, when I was trained as a designer, I learned how to think for myself. I stopped following trends, and rather followed my own sense of style. I learned what looks good and decent on my body as opposed to wearing the latest new-season drop. What I had discovered was my sense of personal style. One of the many benefits of developing my personal style was that I am now able to purchase clothing that I love, usually at a sale price. Because my personal style is more important to me than the latest fashion, my clothes last a lot longer than one season. I also make sure that when I buy clothing, I will be able to wear it to Mass. That is my personal standard when I purchase clothing.

Below are some tips that you could apply to your own life to try to live out a modest lifestyle. Now, these are quite general, but they should begin to generate certain thoughts for you on how to develop your own sense of style:

1. Remember that humility is key. A great personality will always shine through better than any material items you have or don't have. Your belongings do not define you as a person. Rather, they should be complimentary to your personality.

2. Wear clothing that makes you feel confident. If something doesn't fit right, it will show, especially if you are uncomfortable. I am not saying you should

wear a potato sack that covers your entire body. You should wear clothing that fits you and flatters your shape. Everyone is made uniquely, so clothes that are created in one stock standard size cannot be classified as 'for everyone'. Size up if needed as sizing charts rarely follow the same size standards, even within one fashion label. Remember that people will be looking at the clothing you are wearing, not the tag!

3. Understand your effect as a consumer. Something only sells if it is in demand. If you are demanding things that are perceived as modest, the company selling these clothes will take notice. These are the items that are usually re-sold in a new colour, print or tweaked slightly for the upcoming season.

Chapter 36

Dressing like a Catholic man

Like many people living across both urban and rural cities, I have often encountered Mormons, Jehovah's Witnesses, and Protestant door-preachers, and possibly even some belonging to other new-age religions. To my observation over the past decade, they have most certainly been well-dressed, both in formal and smart casual wear. Upon opening the door at each ringing of the doorbell, growing up, my first impression was of their great effort. It wasn't so much the effort to visit the entire neighbourhood block, but rather the effort of dressing in stylish and respectable clothing. I had no choice in my first encounter but to take the sales pitch and to engage them in conversation. This left a very strong impression on me as a young teenager — that men wearing suits and ties would often be perceived more positively than those who just wore casual clothing.

Often, dressing modestly and being well-presented is depicted as a task for women, but nothing could be further from the truth. Both males and females have an equal calling to dress modestly, which is imperative for all people, especially if you wish to be God's representative in the world. If you have ever noticed how sales representatives and Mormons present themselves, you will find that they are both seeking the same outcome, but just with a different product.

Dressing well as a Catholic man will not only encourage people to take you more seriously and make you command more respect, you will also be able to facilitate better evangelisation in your professional and everyday discourse. Remember the shirt, pants and shoes that you wear will allow people to either open up to you and trust you, or to judge you from a distance and not engage with you. This is the reality of the world, which I do not have the answers for. Men's bodies speak a language of strength, sacrifice and giving. You need to dress in line with your personality, which will speak that language in your actions.

Now that, hopefully, you are convinced, you should re-shape your wardrobe, or just simply alter your outfit when at work or in public.

Let's now talk about the importance of dressing a little bit better for Mass on Sunday. The same principle applies for when you are attending the wedding of a family or friend where you feel the need to dress well because there is a presumed dress code. Why is this the case? The simple answer is to show your respect to the bride and groom, because it shows that you respect the solemnity of the event enough to take it seriously, and hence to wear the formal clothing that would demonstrate your sacrifice and effort. There is a serious element of sacrifice for men in dressing and presenting well, especially for Mass.

So here are some fundamental guidelines for any Catholic man to discern and optimise his dress code, so as not to be taken for granted by appearance:

1. When picking an outfit for Mass, wear shirts or pants that you would not wear during the week. Designate Sunday Mass clothes. In the warmer months it could be any collared shirt with more formal jeans or trousers. In winter, try to wear a jacket, blazer or coat to Mass.

2. Put on your outfit. Then proceed before a mirror, and ask yourself: 'Is this how God would want me representing Him before other people, given that I will meet his duty of one-to-one evangelisation?' The reality is, if you are wearing flip-flops and a casual shirt, people will never view your opinion or message as seriously as they would that of a more elegantly dressed person.

3. You may have physical aspects as a man that you are proud of, for example bigger arms, because of your progress with weights. As a useful mortification when selecting an outfit, wear something which is less appealing but still appropriate for the occasion. In other words, do not let pride overtake your decisions when dressing for Mass. Remember, your clothing will influence the way that you feel about yourself and your overall mindset. When I am in comfortable home clothing, my mindset changes from when I wear smart casual clothing for my day job.

Chapter 37

Balancing your 'church involvement'

We have all at one stage of our lives experienced the overly-enthusiastic and heavily involved person in our Catholic community. They are at every event around the city, every parish Bible study, serving every possible public Mass and even running your Sunday morning tea. May God bless these people for their dedication and time to meet the needs of the Church; and I highly commend everyone who puts their youth and time into ensuring Church activities are attended to and are well organised. I strongly advocate that people invest time in the Church's activities and the work of God, instead of all the pointless time that is invested in browsing social media and playing video games. If we spent half the time that Catholics spend on social media working instead for the catechesis or parish fundraiser, we would definitely see great results.

However, I often wonder — and it remains none of my business — whether the prayer lives of these people who are involved in every parish event are identical to the efforts of the fundraisers and committee meetings? If the effort that people place in apostolates and other faith-filled activities is an excuse from spending more time with family, what is their direct moral obligation? The third question I ponder is whether the third Bible study or group for the week is indeed worth my time after all, when I could be working on much more efficacious projects for the salvation of souls?

We must remember that Our Lord may deny knowing us at the end of our lives, if we don't truly have the right intentions for the faith's extracurricular activities in place. Remember, we can't be everywhere and do everything. We need to find a balance between keeping busy and optimising our priorities, from our direct moral obligations such as family and vocation, to allocating Church apostolates and other extracurricular activities.

This chapter details a very serious observation that I have formed over the past decade. I hope the three following tips will help you discern if you are that overly-involved Church events person who needs to redirect your time or put your energy towards other areas that would be more beneficial, as a practising member of the faithful seeking holiness:

1. When an opportunity to take charge of an event or initiative arrives, pray and discern first if the hours will all be efficiently directed for the glory of God and the salvation of souls, and not just towards the activity itself. For example, compare running a stall on Sunday for baked goods versus running a catechesis class. Weigh up the benefits for Our Lord, and the usefulness of your time and energy, and then decide.

2. Allocate others to the relevant positions. If you have discerned not to take charge of an event, check to see if others who have not taken leadership positions previously would spiritually benefit from serving in this way and allocate them to the position. For

example, there may be a parish project that requires people who work well with youth, finance and liturgy. The correct people who are willing and would benefit the position the most should be allocated this project, instead of one person undertaking all tasks. This would distribute the time and energy, while simultaneously engaging many people.

3. Keep yourself in check. Every month, review your time allocated and reassess and make the required changes, if necessary, to reduce or increase your commitment levels to the faith on a pastoral level. What you need to achieve is to prioritise your vocational calling, and use as much time as possible to devote to the apostolate. The order of priority based on your moral obligations must come into play. For example, your family, job, and care needs would need to be first attended to in the true spirit of the Gospel. Then you would naturally proceed to incorporate on a monthly basis additional commitments to the parish and other apostolates, and discern if you will actually add any value there.

Chapter 38

Living true humility in all things

Humility in the name of anything these days is something you will definitely come across in your discourse of Church life. Great judgmentalism can often arise as a result of assuming that degrading one's self, living below one's means, and not boasting about achievements is the exemplification of humility. However, the principle of humility is much richer and broader.

For us to better appreciate and finally master humility in our personal lives, let us turn to paragraph 2559 of the Catechism of the Catholic Church:

> *Prayer is the raising of one's mind and heart to God or the requesting of good things from God. But when we pray, do we speak from the height of our pride and will, or 'out of the depths' of a humble and contrite heart? He who humbles himself will be exalted; humility is the foundation of prayer. Only when we humbly acknowledge that 'we do not know how to pray as we*

> *ought', are we ready to receive freely the gift of prayer. 'Man is a beggar before God'.*

In conclusion, humility is a health balance, or the term, 'humility equilibrium', which seeks to balance accepting that God has given you gifts that you are to use for his glory, without taking that same glory for yourself intentionally, but to only will and act for the glory of God. Accepting and being proud of yourself for spiritual or personal achievements is not an act of pride, but you should ensure that you carry on your review and reflect upon this so you do not miss opportunities because your head was buried in the sand due to pride. Pride is something that limits your ability to conform yourself to God's will and to worship God. There is a reason this is one of the seven deadly sins, and the very cause of the fall of Lucifer himself (Isaiah 14:12-17). In essence, the existence of Lucifer's pride in not humbling himself to serve humanity was the cause of the fall altogether. We could naturally conclude through the course of daily life that all sins and failures have some element of pride within them.

1. Check how your prayer life is progressing every week. I highly recommend doing this during a weekly planning time or a meditation session. Your life of humility will be directly proportional to your prayer life, as we have previously discussed. Your week-plan is absolutely crucial; some people engineer a monthly forecast or plan, but for this the session would require perhaps over an hour, and you may even potentially miss crucial dates or events in your calendar.

2. Do not seek to 'prove' yourself all the time to God in your mindset. The reason you need God's grace is because you are a fallen creature. Keep yourself in check for any spiritual victories, and ensure they were carried out by the grace of God with your cooperation, rather than your egotism and pride. Often during victories, we can take the credit away from the Holy

Spirit and believe that it was purely our skills alone that allowed us to achieve wonders.

3. Achieve the 'humility equilibrium' of balancing this virtue in every life project or within any context. Humility is a perfect balance of adhering to God's word and worshipping by simply conforming oneself to His will, which in turn would have you adjust yourself and your lifestyle.

Chapter 39

Making sense and living canon law

Canon Law (1983) is not one of the prettiest and most attractive aspects of Church life for many people. That is why it is often seen as repressive or dull in the eyes of many younger generations and in the secular media. However, that is why it is necessary to devote some time to actually understanding the purpose of the Code of Canon Law and why it is in our benefit to take heed of and follow, as good and faithful servants of the Church. There can be nothing more practical in its application of the faith, in all areas of the Church, both spiritual and temporal, than the very law and norms that govern her earthly existence.

Our Lord lays the foundation of the authority of the apostles in Mathew 18:18: *'Truly I tell you, whatever you bind on earth will be bound in heaven, and whatever you loose on earth will be loosed in heaven'*.

We are also aware that in the Old Testament the high priests exercised some earthly jurisdiction over the people, where this very concept of ruling over the faithful of God in an earthly sense derives from. Furthermore, if we look at the first council of Jerusalem in the Book of Acts 15:19-20:

> *It is my judgment, therefore, that we should not make it difficult for the Gentiles who are turning to God. Instead we should write to them, telling them to abstain from food polluted by idols, from sexual immorality, from the meat of strangled animals and from blood.*

What we notice is that this is a decree of the council that accompanies the theological clarification that circumcision is not required by Christians. This is the very first taste we have of what we now know as Canon Law. These are earthly laws that pertain to practising the faith and also the administration of all aspects of the Church, which in the same sense as doctrine itself, is binding to all the faithful, but can also be changed over time. An example of this ability to change is that we no longer need to refrain from food 'polluted by idols' (Acts 15:20). There were also changes to the forms of liturgical rituals, such as the form of Mass and other administrative measures in the Church.

So how can we allow this sometimes unappealing and dull law to apply to our lives and enrich our faith? I have the following suggestions for making practical resolutions:

1. See the earthly law of the Church as more beneficial than the secular law on earth. If we must obey traffic laws and the law of the land to better our quality of life, then how much more necessary will abiding by the earthly laws of the Church be, to facilitate and compliment your spiritual life?

2. Read sections of the Code of Canon Law 1983 over time, and understand each canon and write down any questions you may have, and then proceed to consult your parish priest or canonical expert for answers. It is definitely a great part of your life, understanding the kingly authority of Christ

and his Church, that even in temporal matters and earthly dealings, it does indeed deserve our assent.

3. In your prayer, thank God for the order he has placed within human nature. Also reflect for a few minutes and imagine a Church with no structure or laws in place for its temporal or earthly affairs. Would we be able to administer to the poor, the needy and the many souls who seek the Church?

Chapter 40

Always being prepared for death

This is nobody's favourite conversation to have. I firmly believe that without looking at the start of your life and discovering your vocation and mission, you will not be able to approach the future with confidence. The future on earth would look rather ugly and frustrating if it was not capped by the Creator with a timeframe. Think about when you are given a task to complete without a timeframe. The task and the effort seem to become inefficient and drag on for too long, and may never be completed. However, given that you are alive to read this book, you are given a timeframe in which to serve God and achieve His will in a limited amount of time.

Let us make some sense of the reality of death through paragraph 1010 of the Catechism of the Catholic Church:

> *Because of Christ, Christian death has a positive meaning: "For me to live is Christ, and to die is gain". The saying is sure: if we have died with him,*

> *we will also live with him. What is essentially new about Christian death is this: through Baptism, the Christian has already 'died with Christ' sacramentally, in order to live a new life; and if we die in Christ's grace, physical death completes this 'dying with Christ' and so completes our incorporation into him in his redeeming act.*

'Memento mori' is a famous term that describes keeping watch at the hour of death. The very concept of death to someone who has a living faith should turn their thoughts and focus to the legacy that they will leave here on earth. How will you work every day of your life to ensure the salvation of your soul? What legacy do you want to leave here on earth for the people of God? How will you conduct your secular and Church work in a way that gives glory to God, brings people to Christ and allows those with Christ to grow deeper in His love? Furthermore, how will you ensure that the work of God that you have conducted on earth will live on after you depart this world physically?

Let us always be prepared for death sufficiently and always have the necessary hope that lies within us, and we will therefore testify unto (1 Peter 3:15) through the following steps:

1. Morning and evening give thanks to God in our prayer for allowing us to remain alive and for giving us a new day. I believe a small daily reminder will allow us to stay mindful of our mortality and not be overly attached to this world. This practice will aid us infinitely.

2. A daily examination of conscience before bed will allow you to assess if you have committed any mortal sins, venial sins or whether you have any attachment to sin. Then, appropriate resolutions written down every night will allow you to approach the next

day with confidence and a renewed commitment to improving where you have spiritually failed.

3. Set your goals for God and remember in that precise moment by pausing, praying and asking God to give you the grace to complete every task during your lifetime. It is good to remember that the reason you wish to have a longer time on earth is to increase your labour productivity in his earthly vineyard.

Conclusion

To never lose hope ahead

The very essence of taking the law of God found in Scripture, tradition and the Magisterium of the Church is a very difficult and genuine struggle experienced by every single saint throughout history. What makes it even harder to find practical ways to implement this in the life of the Church today is the vast ambiguity in recognising the purpose and mission of the Church. This has unfortunately crippled the clergy and lay faithful to a much lower standard of expectation and execution.

Our focus as a community of *The Catholic Toolbox* is to re-catechise the faithful. This has been a mission in itself, and the people of God (in many cases) are not exposed to taking the faith to the next level and living it spiritually in their actions; liturgically and pastorally. This is the reason why I call this the 'second dimension of the Church's crisis'. Often, many clergy and lay faithful have recognised the signs and symptoms, yet could not put their finger on the problem and how to address it. This is why this movement of finding practical strategies to target catechetical, pastoral, spiritual and liturgical problems has arisen.

How will we have the courage to continue and keep a strong mindset when we may experience discouragement? How are we to assist Holy Mother Church and its members in their varying capacities to implement the faith on a practical level? How do we become like the Word Himself, Jesus Christ, to reach the goal and homeland in mind — heaven for all eternity? What I will touch on will be the collective experience of all faithful Catholics of this millennium.

It is important to understand the climate that you will be facing when you begin to adhere to living your faith more radically in the ordinary world. This is a climate of hostile secularism and simultaneously one of desire for truth by some who have been led astray into the darkness of the world. May I bring your attention to the Easter Vigil liturgy, particularly the entrance of the paschal candle into the darkened church. This is the exact analogy that describes the phenomenon of the change of attitude required. You must be a bearer of the light of Christ through both learning and living your faith, thereby practically executing the evangelical endeavours in your daily life as you act as an ambassador of the light, and an ambassador of Christ himself.

Preparing our faith's future after coronavirus

The social climate during this time of the coronavirus pandemic leaves us with uncertainty about the future. However, I truly believe that there is a great degree of certainty about what will be the social situation and norms to come in the next few years and for the new age ahead. What we are definitely seeing now is a large shift from the traditional office structure to an open working space and inevitably a remote office from one's home. This can definitely be more convenient for people, however, this also has deep implications about the way we are able to bear witness to Christ in the future.

I urge you to invest some time in creating or enhancing one or more social media platforms so that you are able to bring the Gospel to those around you. This may be colleagues, distant friends and even your fellow members of the faith-filled community. This is definitely an era of more isolation from the real world and perhaps a virtual presence. This is where we must constantly have a flexible mindset to adapt to the means we have to reach others, to whatever upgrades are implemented to our way of life. This is no different from every other generation that adapted to the use of electricity, microphones, computers or any other means of communication or social enhancement.

Furthermore, my uncertain prediction is that there will be great appreciation for a 'true presence' among family and friends in general after this pandemic has passed. Even towards the more distant future, where day-to-day life will become more remote, people will value the real presence of people, and most especially the holy Mass. I believe we will see a refreshed Church, and a more vibrant community, with a great hunger for the faith. This will be attributed to the self-isolation measures imposed by worldwide governments. However, I have always been optimistic during this time of uncertainty. It was the uncertainty and isolation that catalysed the faith of the early Church, and the faith of Christians today in the Middle East who have been relentlessly persecuted. Though we are not in a situation of persecution, I do hold to the reality that there is a common denominator, that of uncertainty and isolation from the Christian community, both in the context of the Mass and gatherings.

Here are a few key points that you can refer back to when you are struggling to live the faith and to help the body of Our Lord and its members live the faith when they have despaired, have become complacent or when giving up is being employed as a practical strategy by the enemy:

1. Take a step back, pray and remember that it is not your work that is being carried out, but rather it is God's work. For example, we may not see physical results in parish catechesis attendance or the levels of virtue which have grown in your life at times. The downside is a sign that perhaps the strategy may need to be revised or re-implemented better. Remember that it is a learning curve.

2. Remember that it took 40 years for the Church to see the unmentionable statistics, and will take another 10 to 20 years to see some serious recovery in numbers. So be realistic in your expectations, but also balance your expectations with higher ones to meet better targets, and don't fear failure.

3. Turn to your spiritual director and seek counsel to bounce back from any signs of despair. Remember we have nothing to lose anymore, Our Lord has won the battle, and the Church throughout history undergoes purification and will recover once again. The choice is yours in how you will now play your part in living your faith and how you will re-implement the faith practically.

The Ten Commandments:

1. I am the LORD your God. You shall worship the Lord your God and Him only shall you serve.

2. You shall not take the name of the Lord your God in vain.

3. Remember to keep holy the Sabbath day.

4. Honor your father and your mother.

5. You shall not kill.

6. You shall not commit adultery.

7. You shall not steal.

8. You shall not bear false witness against your neighbour.

9. You shall not covet your neighbour's wife.

10. You shall not covet your neighbour's goods.

Prayer to St Michael the Archangel

St. Michael the Archangel, defend us in battle, be our protection against the wickedness and snares of the devil. May God rebuke him we humbly pray; and do thou, O Prince of the Heavenly host, by the power of God, cast into hell Satan and all the evil spirits who prowl about the world seeking the ruin of souls. Amen.

Recommended Reading

Archbishop. M. Sheehan, *Apologetics and Catholic Doctrine* (The Saint Austin Press, London, revised by Father Peter Joseph, 2010).

Deacon Harold Burke-sivers, *Behold the Man: A Catholic Vision of Male Spirituality* (Ignatius Press, 2015).

Father John Flader, *A Tour of the Catechism - The Creed* (Connor Court Publishing, 2011).

Father John Flader, *Journey into Truth - Instructions in the Catholic Faith* (Connor Court Publishing, 2014).

Father John Flader, *Question Time 1: 150 Questions and Answers on the Catholic Faith* (Connor Court Publishing, 2008).

Father John Flader, *Question Time 2: 150 Questions and Answers on the Catholic Faith* (Connor Court Publishing, 2012).

Father John Flader, *Question Time 3: 150 Questions and Answers on the Catholic Faith* (Connor Court Publishing, 2016).

Father John Flader, *Question Time 4: 150 Questions and Answers on the Catholic Faith* (Connor Court Publishing, 2018).

Father John Flader, *Question Time 5: 150 Questions and Answers on the Catholic Faith* (Connor Court Publishing, 2020).

Karl Keating, *Catholicism and Fundamentalism* (Ignatius Press, 1988).

Ludwig Ott, *Fundamentals of Catholic Dogma* (The Mercier Press, Ltd., 1958).

Scott Hahn (and Benjamin Wiker), *Answering the New Atheism: Dismantling Dawkins's Case Against God* (Emmaus Road Publishing, 2008).

Scott Hahn, *Rome Sweet Home* (co-written with Kimberley Hahn), (Ignatius Press, 1993).

Scott Hahn, *The Lamb's Supper: The Mass as Heaven on Earth* (Doubleday, 1999).

Stephen K. Ray, *Crossing the Tiber* (Ignatius Press, 1997).

About *The Catholic Toolbox*

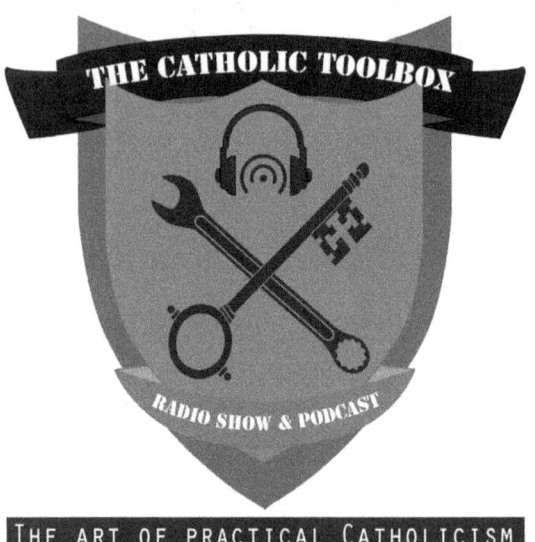

(Radio show, podcast and consultancy)
www.thecatholictoolboxshow.com

The Catholic Toolbox is a radio show and podcast founded by George Manassa and Akita Sanchez, which is broadcast on Voice of Charity Australia (1701AM Sydney) and CRadio online (cradio.org.au). It also delivers public talks on various topics of the faith, customised to the needs of our modern world, equipping listeners with practical solutions to live and directly implement their faith personally in our modern world.

Off-air, it is also a consultancy service, existing to respond to what it calls 'the second dimension of the Church's crisis' — the lack of the practical application of the faith. *The Catholic Toolbox* consultancy has advised parishes, chaplaincies, apostolates and other Catholic organisations in making direct amendments to the enhancement of their catechesis, liturgical life and pastoral outreach — all in keeping up-to-date with the ongoing changes to the social condition and needs of our modern world.

If your parish, chaplaincy, apostolate or organisation requires assistance in enhancing its performance via a private or public consultation, why not consider an independent and autonomous advisory? We believe that external analysis of the problems facing Catholic organisations in effectively carrying out the work of God can be better addressed using an external advisor. This provides both an objective and detailed diagnosis of obstacles to evangelical underperformance, addressed only thereafter by practical solutions and strategies, to achieve effective outcomes, resulting in the salvation of souls.

About *The Rite of Manhood*

www.theriteofmanhood.com

The Rite of Manhood is a podcast and growing community established by George Manassa and Akita Sanchez to provide men with practical ways to become and grow as men in our modern world. The podcast can be downloaded on all available networks.

On our podcast and community, we also work with women to help men become better fathers, husbands, brothers or sons. The role of women in the development of boys to become virtuous and actual men is vital. This is not about a gender war or any competition for dominance; rather, this is both genders working equally to help each other become who they are for society in all the different levels of relationships that actually demand men to be men.

You can join this project, which is setting out to restore man to his former glory, by assisting to pave the way to create a rite of passage, which can only take place once after the accumulation of skills in all areas of life, and after proficiency and mastery of them; to then finally earn the title of being a man; and then growing in this way of life and becoming the best version of yourself. It is vital that the concept of masculinity is not just discussed in principle, without any practical guidelines, in order to take action immediately.

The three values by which every man must live, and which describe the very nature of what is embedded within the male attributes are to lead, protect and provide. These core values are the litmus test for calling oneself a man, and must be mastered. If we think about it, these three aspects summarise everything you could actually think about within the testosterone-filled creature that prowls the earth, and I will now elaborate on that further:

Lead

To master the fine art of leadership in any aspect of your life, whether it's work, family, the Church or within yourself, it is a prerequisite that you must have carried out what you are leading in. That is to say, you start right at the bottom as a groundsman, not to imply that hierarchy represents leadership in and of itself.

Three practical tips to actually lead and lead well:

1. Strong communication with all parties.
2. Demonstrate what needs to be carried out by example.
3. Let others' light shine and do not desire the credit interiorly.

Protect

This one gets a bit of a bad misrepresentation. Protection comes in many forms within the context of being a man. Physically, we men receive testosterone, which provides them with an objectively stronger physique than females. This is to be used for serving others. The male anatomy itself represents the purpose it exists for, to protect from danger, to fight wars, to work and labour to provide. However, we can be an emotional wreck to others sometimes through our negativity, which is where the symbol of the rose here at *The Rite of Manhood* comes in, representing the chivalry and gentleness of men. In summary, we protect physically, emotionally, and socially from bad company and from every area of life. We cannot simply cover every practical scenario.

Provide

Providing is probably one of the most controversial topics within our gender-confused society today. However, I would just like to clarify that both men and women should have equal opportunity for working and earning the same income. That is not to say that someone should earn more or be given an unfair advantage, because of gender, because that would in essence disrespect the person and their gender.

So providing, for men, is definitely for the financial aspect, of bringing the bread to the table to feed one's self, one's family and to assist in the community. Men are called to provide spirituality through any form of religion, socially through helping others and one's family network with others, and finally providing input of common sense and skill to social situations — essentially being useful wherever it is needed. That is why we might call someone a handyman. What I am saying is to essentially be a handyman in every aspect of life.

Partners

The Voice of Charity Australia (1701AM)
www.voc.org.au

Parousia Media
www.parousiamedia.com.au

Cradio
www.cradio.org.au

Kreim Media
www.kreimmedia.org.au

Notes and Practical Resolutions

Notes and Practical Resolutions

Notes and Practical Resolutions

Notes and Practical Resolutions

Notes and Practical Resolutions

About the Author

George Manassa is the host and founder of *The Catholic Toolbox* radio show, podcast and consultancy. Co-founded with creative director Akita Sanchez, the program has a large audience and provides practical strategies for Catholic individuals and organisations to implement their faith personally and to improve evangelical  performance around Sydney and NSW. George is also the founder of *The Rite of Manhood* podcast, drawing in men of all faiths united for a common purpose, which is to restore masculinity today.

Inspired by the spirituality of St Josemaria Escriva, George has spent the past decade working in project management to bring God to the secular world in the midst of the ordinary circumstances of daily life. This work is targeted to those in the professional, political and social spheres, which seek to drive out faith altogether. A firm believer in delivering results within the construction and property sector, George is trying to fuse these entrepreneurial and business-oriented mindsets to the Church's approach to implement the New Evangelisation effectively now and for the future.

George has presented and spoken publicly on topics such as liturgy, the development of men, Catholic professionalism, Protestantism, Catholic political influence today, prayer and evangelisation. In this book, he seeks to put these topics into a practical perspective, and to strategise for the glory of God.

www.ingramcontent.com/pod-product-compliance
Lightning Source LLC
Chambersburg PA
CBHW051401290426
44108CB00015B/2113